Nectar of Woman

Woman of the Circle...come...

Mary Saint-Marie/Sheoekah

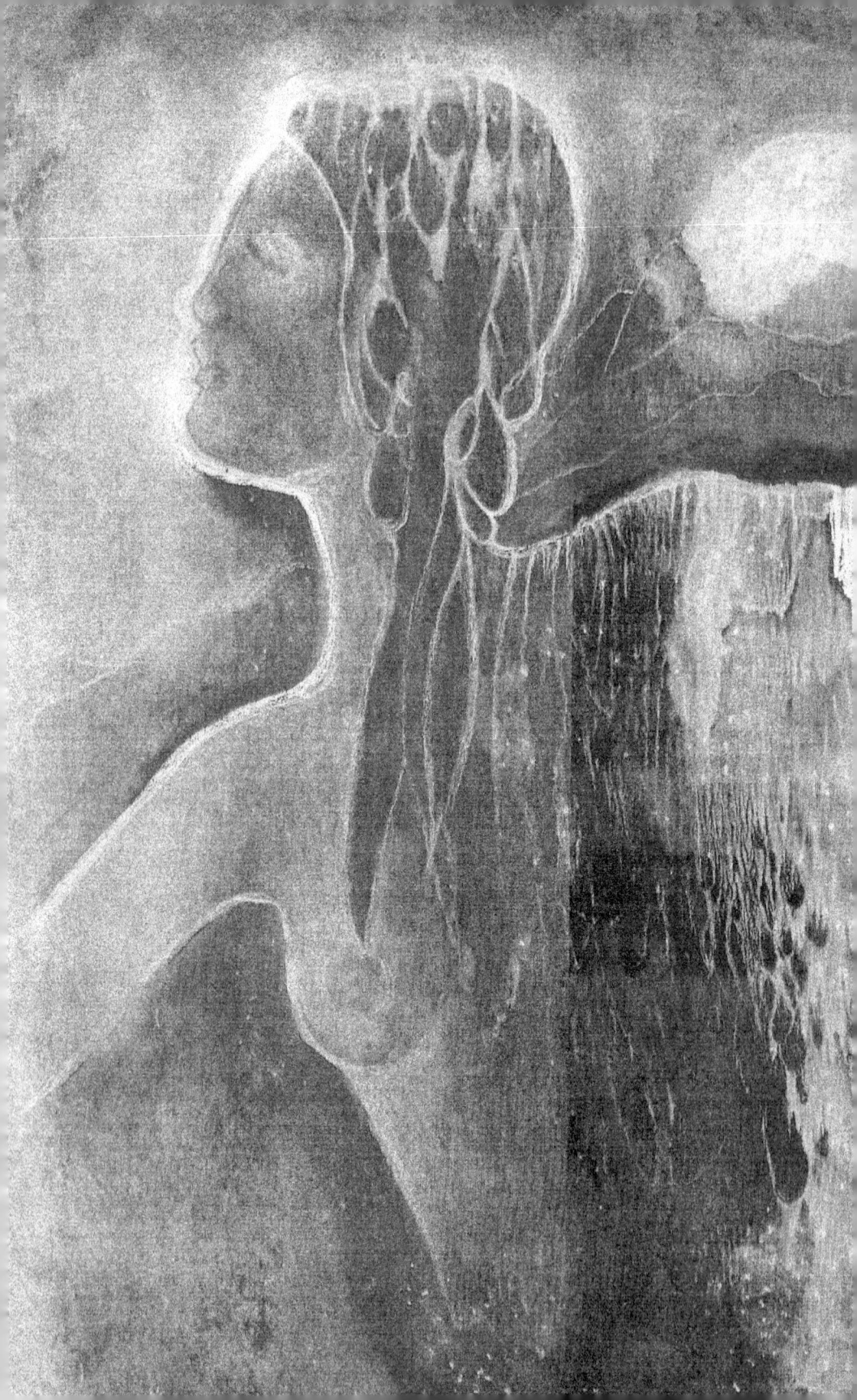

Nectar of Woman

Woman of the Circle...come...

Second Edition, Revised 2015
© 2005, 2015 Mary Saint-Marie / Sheoekah. All Rights Reserved.

No part of this book may be reproduced, stored in a retrieval system, or transmitted by any means without the written permission of the author.

Published by Ancient Beauty Studio, www.marysaintmarie.com

ISBN: 978-0-9646572-7-4 (sc)

Photo Credits: Page 126, 129, and 130, Kris McMillan

Cover Art: *Starry Mantle of Spirit,* by Mary Saint-Marie

Book Design and Layout by Aaron Rose, Mount Shasta, California

Other publications by Mary Saint-Marie:
Galactic Shamanism
The Holy Sight
Messages from the Silence
The Sacred Two
The Star-Stone Ones
The Animating Presence
The Monitor and Laughter of the Gods
Art As Consciousness
The Oracle and the Dreamer

This book is dedicated to the Balance borne of Oneness.

*This book is dedicated to the Feminine Principle
in man and in woman.*

This book is dedicated to Woman…everywhere…

Cover Art and Poem by Mary Saint-Marie

Starry Mantle of Spirit

wandering…throughout eternity…
wearing…starry mantle of spirit…
joy does fill my soul…

Starry Mantle of Spirit reminds us that we are ever cloaked in the Timeless Infinity that speaks only of the exaltation of Oneness.

I thank Spider Woman...
who gently did lift me into her realm...
that fills the sky...

I thank Spider Woman...
who unveiled all women as One woman...

all women...
one woman...
everywoman...

I thank Spider Woman...
who did unveil the One Dance...
the dance...of Beauty-SHE...

Contents

Acknowledgments *11*
Voice of Woman *13*
The Voice of Love *15*
About the Writing Style *17*
Introduction *19*
Preface *25*

Passages of Nectar of Woman

O Woman…come… *29*
Invitation to the Nectar of Woman *31*
Hasten… *33*
Voice of World Mothers *34*
Journey of Balance *42*
Animated by Infinity *48*
Patriarchal Genocide *49*
Charmed *51*
Why has SHE allowed? *56*
Law of Balance *58*
Honor Nature Now *63*
Temple of Darkness *66*
Foresee the Day of Venus *68*

Illumined Creature of the Sea 70

Worth Endless Eternities................................... 77

O Woman…Ask to Know................................. 78

Wordless Songs to the Moon 79

Cauldron of Creator: Amriti of He and She.......... 80

A King without a Queen?.................................. 87

Invitation to Intimacy....................................... 89

Woman as Ransom... 91

Liberation of Love.. 92

Inner Sanctum of True Man and True Woman 93

Safe to Speak 95

Illness: A Call for Change.................................. 96

Monsters in Our Midst No More… 98

O Heaven World... 103

Seedless Society... 105

Fascinated with Pathologies 107

Breakthrough into the Light 113

A Painless World Birth 115

*Marie Saint-Marie: Mystic Artist, Writer,
and Spiritual Educator*......................................127

Mystic Art, Books, Sessions, and Retreats............ 131

Acknowledgments

I wish to thank the women and the men on the planet everywhere, that are opening to the I Am Awareness, that allows the arising of the divine feminine principle to express fully in equal and balanced measure with the divine masculine principle on this precious earth. The Dance of Yin and Yang. The Dance of the One.

I wish to thank the women on the planet that have come to me for many decades to "Hold Sacred Space" for them, as their direct knowing from the Withinness began to arise. What ecstatic joy to witness each one emerge as unique beauty to be expressed.

I am in gratitude to each woman for all that I have also learned, while being in Holy Sight.

I am in gratitude to my two daughters as I watched them blossom into beautiful women and find their own chosen expressions.

I am in gratitude for the living and original archetypes of the Mother of the Home and the Mother of the World. May the teachings of those archetypes continue to touch and guide the emergence of the new earth culture and creations!

I am always moved when Spirit speaks direct to any of us. And I am always in gratitude when we are listening.

And I am ever in gratitude when we move beyond the need for the conversation and dwell in the eternal awareness that IS.

I am grateful for the time to rest in the Timeless Realm that these passages could come into Consciousness.

I wish to thank Laura Daen who listened to these passages as they arrived and responded. It is a gift to have a listener.

I wish to thank Aaron Rose for the designing of this second edition, bringing with him, as he always does, his gift of hearing the soul of the book.

Voice of Woman

This book is a Call to Woman to go inward, into the sacred space where woman is Woman. It is the space, that is a state of Consciousness, where woman realizes herself as Archetypal Woman. It will not come from studies and workshops and books or even teachers. They can point the way. They are poignant preparation for the readiness to go within.

This book is to inspire woman to go within to find the Woman that she is. Already IS!

Now is the time to find that SHE…the True Original Woman… is your very Soul Self.

Now is the time.

Then shall come the actual experience of your True Identity.

Then, the Goddess may emerge.

SHE…awaits our seeing.

The Light of this knowing is within.

The Voice of Love

One of the purposes of this book is to inspire women to use their voices. To allow this voice to express what needs love, nourishment, care and protection. This voice of love must encompass all aspects of life.

Woman can no longer wait and hope others will be the voice for them. Each and every situation and condition that turns up in one's life is the opportunity and the invitation to allow the voice of the divine feminine to be heard. It is the Voice of Love.

And this planet does need this voice. It is the yin part of the yin/yang balance. It is the other half of what needs to be expressed. Now.

The moment one sees the inviolate universal law of balance, which is the law of love, being violated, that is the time for this voice of woman. That is the perfect moment. That is the Timeless message of love arriving in time.

In this book, at the beginning of some of the passages, there is mention of some of the imbalanced conditions on the planet. These passages may be read with great and deep awareness. One will see that they have been written as a literal "passage." They enter the condition and allow needed passage to an elevated understanding and awareness.

It is the elevated consciousness and seeing that opens the door to bring the change.

In the elevated consciousness, one may see the solutions and the ideal to be landed upon this plane. The "as above, so below" is clearly invited.

Woman, find your voice.
Find your Sacred Voice.

Allow it to flow forth.
Allow the voice of love to spread across the globe.
Allow love's expression now.

About the Writing Style

The communions and messages in this book came mainly in the night and pre-dawn and while driving down highways and across deserts. They came to me as poetry, sentences, and poetic odyssey. Sometimes there came only a phrase. Sometimes merely a word.

I have written what came as stream of consciousness. There has been no attempt to shift the messages into a formal writing style. The downpourings come as moving and living essence with form, rhythm, and cadence, that bring in their wake for me great joy and a heightened and illumined awareness. I do my best to share the messages in the virgin state they are received.

Introduction

Woman of the Circle…come…

A Solitary Retreat for Woman: *Nectar of Woman*

The tides are turning; we are witnessing great shifts never seen in history. Woman is announcing herself in a way that is having far-reaching affects.

In 1992, I sold my lovely home at the base of Mt. Shasta; I was guided to travel for three months in the Southwest. As I traveled about, it was revealed that women would begin making the "Passage from Mother of the Home to Mother of the World." I was shown that the world needs a mother, not some mythological woman read about in dusty books, but flesh and blood women who have touched Archetypal Woman, and who now can speak up and act…pouring love across this world in pain…

I was shown that the world we live in will not be balanced until there is man/woman balance across the lands and across the seas. And I was shown that that would not happen until man and woman had found their Balance within.

It was revealed that the planet is in a pregnant moment, that we are birthing:

The World Birth of Balance.

That birth is preceded by a conception borne of a virgin heart.

In that virgin heart is found and known…the Holy Presence.

I have been having dreams since the 1970's where I was dancing with women in the forests and jungles. I was very busy raising children at that time and still hoping to find my partner, that my daughters would have a "daddy." Dreams continued. I wanted to be with my partner, so I could not understand why dreams of "dancing with the women" were coming.

Tell the Women…

Then by 1997, "messages to woman" began to come. Intense and powerful messages began to come. They revealed in strong language to the women that it was time. Repeatedly, I heard inwardly…*Tell the Women*. Until this time, I have only read these messages to ones doing Soul Sessions and Retreats with me and to several friends, who continue to reply that each has been so timely and potent in their own situation and has been an answer to prayer. They have also informed me that they could "feel the energy" of the transmission that had come to me on a current of light. In the heightened awareness, of the downpouring of the messages, comes the wordless rapture of the soul.

These "messages to woman" have come to inspire woman to find her "inner strength," her inner knowing, that she may live from her Wholeness of Self, that she may enact from her True Identity, not from the external world of fear based on false premise.

These "messages to woman" initiate a passage:

Passage from Mother of the Home to Mother of the World

It is time…
Woman…it is time…
Now is the Time…

Woman, coming forth at this time, as True Original Woman, will catalyze the changing of the ages. It will catalyze the birthing of the World Birth of Balance.

It sounds like a deep and serious message. Quite the contrary. This passage of women as a collective brings beauty, joy, and laughter as never before known, for it brings the open heart of Presence.

It brings the virgin heart, unladen with human concepts and fear. It brings unprecedented outpourings of love and caring for all. That all…includes the Earth and her precious inhabitants, the animals, the plants, the minerals. It includes the sky and the water.

It will be known widely that the world needs a Mother. World Mother. She will act through flesh and blood. No longer will she be relegated to mythic study.

Mother of the World

Woman, you are the Mother of the World.
Allow her to live and breathe and love through you.
Allow her to have her way.
Allow her to enact…

This is simply, very simply…Presence…Holy Presence…through woman.

Allow that woman now…

These messages have come in a form I never imagined nor asked for. I know that they come forth now to inspire women to find their own voice and expression and strength…that awaits within.

In imbalance, is fear, pain, suffering, and a continued subservience and slavery and impotence. Woman is not becoming equal to man; she is Already equal. Live out from that knowing as a "Goddess of Reciprocity!" Already Am!

Woman…it is time…arise.

Arise…knowing yourself as Presence, as Spirit, as Source, as the Nothingness that fills all space, as the bringer of beauty and joy, and the protectress of purity.

Arise and find yourself.

Arise and help woman everywhere be aware of this Presence. Help them in the collective birthing of the Divine Feminine Principle.

Help woman everywhere to trust her heart.
It speaks to them.
It guides them.

It is time.
This World Birth of Balance may be a painless birth.
Let us begin this day…
Woman of the Circle…come…

I have worked with many hundreds of women from around the world in Soul Sessions since 1985. I offer now these passages as a solitary retreat, making use of these "messages to woman."

In Presence...
does end the drama of duality...

In Presence...
does end the never ending human sagas of sorrow...

In Presence...
does end the habits of humanity...

In Presence...
does woman find no need to play helpless and unknowing...

In Presence...
does woman find a new awareness of independence...

In Presence...
does woman tip humanity's scales...

In Presence...
woman does bring the children Home...

In Presence...
finally smiles do come in the wake of true freedom...
grace...

Preface

After years of working with many hundreds of women from around the world, these passages and stream of consciousness writings began to float in upon my awareness.

I had no idea at first why they were arriving in my Awareness in moments of the great quiet. They began in 1997 and ended in 2005.

At one point it was clear that they were to inspire women into the inner space of the One Power, of the One Consciousness. Of the Essence World. In its wake, this Essence births the transcendent Dance of the Yin and Yang, in equal measure, upon this precious plane of existence. The Balance of masculine/feminine that has eluded humanity is the Love Essence of all of Nature. The Universal Law of Balance. And finally the Dance of the One. In full freedom and wild display!

Some of the women I work with have become very yang in order to make it in their perceived world. Those women desire to realize that inner One more deeply, so that the yin of their being may lead the way. And their feminine emerges and expresses freely. Soul Expression becomes their life. Shapeshifting and being the Fullness.

Other women feel suppressed, depressed, oppressed. They feel the external pressure of the dominant yang paradigm keeping them in their cramped cage. When they finally identify with the One Power within and feel and allow the immense inner calling for Soul Expression, their lives change, shift, and are wildly authentic. Unprecedented.

Woman that are one with the One Power are bringers of the feminine values of love, caring, nourishing, nurturing, culture, beauty. The arts and beauty are no longer denigrated by a mental yang world, nor are they prescribed by society. Original emerges! Raw and indigenous original emerges!

What is spoken here is beyond the concept of empowerment for women. There is but One Power. Not man power and woman power. In competition. In conflict. In opposition. Simply the One Power…animating all!

As men and women everywhere stay vigilant in the realizing of the Self as the One Power, the transcendent Dance of the One may ensue with ease, for that is the River of Life, and it is the great unknown!

Passages of Nectar of Woman

O Woman...come...

O woman...you think you long for man...the one...
You think you search ever for a lover, a boyfriend, a husband...
You think you search ever for the man you are with to "see" you,
to acknowledge you, to honor you...

O woman...I tell you true.
You search in vain.
You search only for your Self...

O woman...come...after these long eons...
break the longing...break the addiction...
of this illusion...

O woman...find the One within...
Find the Self of you...
that is ever your beloved...

Lover and beloved...finally one...
the two as One...
I tell you...find that One...

All else shall come. All else.
Even...the outer one...the man...
even He shall find his way to your door...

For He can't help himself...
arriving as a reflection of She...

He and She...joined within...
and appearing in the place you know as world...

O woman…walk away from the addiction…the illusion…
find the marriage in your heart…

The sacred marriage…it awaits…
O woman…come…

3-13-2005, just after dawn in Taos

Invitation to the Nectar of Woman

Woman…the ability to work,
earn financial freedom, vote, or give opinions
is not "full freedom"…

Woman…is a spiritual force…
To be True Woman…that force…that power…
must be unleashed…from within…
not just over bridge or bingo…
but in all avenues…
in all individual expressions…
in all cultural expressions…

Woman…let us begin…

We are that living story…

We are that living revelation…
Let us rejoice in that knowing…

We are the living Nectar…
Let us drink deeply from the cup…
Let us devour life on our plate…

Joy does call your name…
Are you listening to the wind through the trees?

Woman…are you asking?
How do I release this Nectar?

Woman is a flower with
effervescing fragrance…

Woman need do nothing…
but allow the Nectar of Spirit
flow through in each move,
each glance…each sound of light…

Woman…True Woman…is Essence of Nectar…
and she does light the Way…

She…it is…who brings her children Home…

Woman…are you asking?
Where is that Home?

It is within and its distance is incalculable…
for it dwells outside of time and space…
And it is unapproachable…
for it is not directional…
And it is unspeakable…
for it escapes the mind…
It escapes the mind that would dissect it into nothing…

Well…it is the Nothing…
it is the Nothing that is the Everything…
it is "todo y nada"…

Woman…let us bring the children Home…
Bring the children Home…

9-7-2003, while driving from Taos to Los Angeles

Hasten...

Friends, we think the problem is
this government or that government.
We think it is this nation or that nation.
Or even this politician or that politician.

I tell you friends, we must dig deeper.
Far deeper, I tell you, far deeper...
We must dig for the treasure...
Find it waiting as the foundation of culture.
Religions, traditions, and priesthoods
have torn us from the treasure.

That treasure is balance.
It does sing
and it does dance...
for it is not in opposition.

Man and woman, in balance, my friends...
I tell you...it is simple.
And I tell you again and yet again...
until woman does rise,
leaving forever her cage and broken wings...
humanity will not rise...
culture will not bloom...

Let us hasten...while the sun is high in the sky.
Let us hasten...while yet there is light.

11-12-2004, while driving to Santa Fe

Voice of World Mothers

Western culture loves to hear scholarly treatises and scientific theories and philosophical reasons and arguments. But who wants to hear about the feelings and emotions of intuition that woman has? It is denigrated as sentiment and over sensitivity and emotionalism.

Western world has home-fathers and world-fathers. And it has home-mothers, but few world-mothers. It has women that speak just like the man-world, but truly we have few World Mothers. They are birthing now and coming forth.

They are giving equal voice to create a World of Balance. We need World Mothers that will speak directly from the heart and soul, of feelings and knowings, and not need to travel the mental round of reasons and arguments and endless fruitless interpretations.

Women must begin to reveal that we don't need reasons. We only need to know. There is that mysterious knowing that cannot be explained, so it has been laughed at, ridiculed, suppressed, annihilated, ignored, and disgraced.

The so-called elite have created snobbism around IQ's and PhD's. It is time that we balance the scales. It is time to realize that "truth" can be known direct through intuition without tons of mental debris.

Just look at the Western world to see if the methods of mental play solved our global or local problems and created a safe and caring culture of great nobility. We are savage, cruel, and barbaric. It is just that no one wants to say it.

In regard to treatment of the animals in zoos, factory farms, research experiments, entertainment, and even in the wild, it does not take a PhD, a scientist, or a philosopher to tell any of us of the miscreations happening, the breaking of the one inviolate Law of Love. Children know when an animal is hurting and suffering. So do women. Even a moron does know.

Why do we need to write books to get the patriarchal world to see? Because they are cut off from feeling, from the Soul, from Spirit. As women of Western culture free themselves of fear to speak direct truth from their heart, we will see changes being made.

As women are exposed to the truth of what is happening, they will demand loving care and guardianship of the animals.

Not because of reasons. Because it is felt. It is the truth.

That we would, through the centuries, even have to ask if animals suffer and feel pain is sheer ignorance of the obvious, and denial in the face of clarity. That we have had philosophers from the Age of Reason until the present day try to answer the obvious is absurd, a farce. The ability of the mind to distort, pervert, and twist the truth in clever ways is almost unfathomable to a clear and pure heart and soul. It wants to say simply…let us get Real.

But no, the mind would rather traverse vast fields of games of self-interest, of fascination with pathology and pain, and go on for years and centuries of dwelling in concepts, in beliefs, and casting about for suckers that are taken with brilliant rhetoric. Truly, the mind, disconnected from the heart, is our Fall. The real Fall. The separation.

Psychology and modern medicine would rather travel in realms of research of diseases, disorders, and pathologies, than to study wholeness.

Even in its relationship with animals, the patriarchal world/mind would kill, dissect, and take apart while the heart would admire, observe, appreciate in its wholeness, in its relationship with Nature, its family, the weather. The heart is not sentimental. It is honoring, respectful, revering. It gathers truth from wholeness, not from pain and destruction.

The heart cannot fathom the ignorance of this approach that would violate the obvious Law of Nature…of Balance…of Love. And that would need to maim and harm to gather statistics.

That we need to kill animals to stay healthy is indeed a lie. A grand lie that we have bought. It is time to wake up from the lie. In that call for truth from within, it will be forthcoming in its own way for each individual.

Let us begin.

Let us begin to listen to the Voice of World Mothers. Everywhere. It is a simple voice. A voice of truth and a voice of love.

Philosophers speak of ethics and morality. From where do they think ethics and morality are borne? They are borne of love. Of the heart. Every mother can tell you…and each child.

We turned such simplicity into the science of philosophical reason and arguments, most of which disagree with each other down through the ages and many of whom, throughout history, happen to be men. And with no heart, it would seem.

Ethics and morality are the effect of a culture that knows love, that is at home in the heart. It is not a reasoned position, a rigid stance of the mind pretending to know.

Life is here in many forms. We can love the forms of Life or not. All the forms. Not some of the forms. The patriarchal/mind model has made it all very complicated. And it is not.

When Woman finally gives Voice, she becomes a voice of a Life Giver and a lover of that life in all manner of forms. She loves that life. She nourishes it. She cherishes it. She respects it. She protects it. All manner of form.

>This is the Mother of the Home.
>This is the Mother of the World.

World Mothers care about the air, the water, the earth. They care about the animals, about the plants. They care that they are loved, watched over, protected.

This caring for Nature has been ignored and suppressed and given no value.

No philosopher, scientist, or PhD can fix this imbalanced world with theories and ideas. The world will Balance when it has equal voice for the Woman. It will balance when we have city fathers and city mothers, a king and a queen, a president and presidenta. Man and woman in Balance. Mind and Heart in Balance. It will not happen any other way. Is anybody listening? It will not happen any other way.

Our cultures must take note of Love, of heart, of Balance. There is no other way. The reasoning mind will search on for ages if it wishes; it will never find the Balance in the reasoning mind.

Love and feelings are not a philosophy. They are an experience. They are apart from the mental realms and they form a relationship that is an actual 3-D experience. It need not be talked about, thought about, researched about. It just is.

The thinkers cannot even come close to this experience. They must become receptive, vulnerable, open, receptive…getting very still. Going into the heart, one opens to feel. That is scary. There are no more defenses. Only the opening to direct knowing through the heart and soul.

Our culture will need to learn to give equal value to this direct knowing, to feeling, to intuition.

And that time has come. We can go no further in the imbalance of a mental and patriarchal dominated world that can't figure out what is going on.

For the mind to solve a problem, it must get still…allowing heart and soul to give it Vision and Revelation and Knowing. Then human mind can, as a tool, an instrument, create as much as it wants, for it creates from insight, from truth, from knowing.

Through history, the patriarchy has tried to create from parts, not the whole. It has created from lies and false premises. And philosophers through the ages debate away, with the opinions and beliefs and human concepts cast about, in an effort to give direction to an imbalanced world.

> The mortal mind must have Vision, truth!
> Let us begin.

And if one were an award-winning journalist who could quote from Dostoevski, Thomas Mann, and James Joyce and others of the literary giants of the time, the great minds of history's lore… then one would be listened to. Yes! Yes! She does know. She is knowledgeable. She has a great mind. She has memorized and repeated the great minds of our time.

I say in simplicity. She is a robot. A parrot. Remembering and repeating. Copying. It is not original. She speaks from a trained and conditioned and programmed mind.

Let us hear from Original. Our Origins. Our heart. Let us hear, not through only the trackings of the ever human mind in survival and fear and greed. But let us listen to the direct and simple knowing of the heart. Our culture likes to refer to people who speak in that way as peasants, even simpletons. We have deeply denigrated throughout the ever falling civilizations… simple knowing.

We pretend we need great university degrees to know. I say. It is a lie. It is a lie and we must wake to hear the heart if we would be a culture in Balance. All of Nature knows Balance when there is no interference by a patriarchal mindset.

Woman has great simple truths to offer the patriarchal/mind world. And she rises now to tell Her-Story. It will be told. It is being told. The patriarchal minds who are watching and listening…they…with woman…will pioneer the first real steps of World Balance on a global scale. They will lead the way. They will be wayshowers. They will show that humanity must tap into the Balance displayed by all of Nature when not manipulated and controlled and ravaged and raped by the patriarchal/mind world in separation from Source.

World Mothers carry the message of Oneness in all things. The women carry the message of Balance. And that Oneness will only be experienced in nation upon nation when men and women are in Balance.

That is not to say to adopt a new ideology. A new creation of the clever human mind to control other minds and bodies and cultures. This is very simple. It is the way of Nature. It is the way of harmony and balance. Its results are love…are Oneness.

How is this done, you say? The mystics have been largely ignored by the intellects, the scholarly. But this is the time for the simpleness of the mystics to be revealed. How did they have such rapture, such ecstasy, such peace and inner joy? Few in the ivory towers would ask, for it does not take the great use of the mental powers. It takes solitude. It takes emptiness. It takes contemplation and reflection on truth, on love, on Oneness. Then, in that openness, that receptivity, borne of the feminine principle, life does change. Then begin the revelations, the experiences, the visions of truth, the direct experiences, the changed outer world. O how we have relegated the mystics to a position of "monastery monks." Did we never think that those living those experiences would someday be invited to walk the earth, to mingle in the marketplace, to share their simple message? What did we think these monks were for? Strange anomalies? Impractical dreamers?

So now the world must choose. All must choose. Balance or imbalance. That is the choice. And for those who choose Balance, which is the inviolate law of the universe, they must learn how to find Balance. To learn how to live in the world, we must turn within. We must find the love, the Oneness waiting simply in our hearts. Our ever waiting human mind will translate and interpret these great truths that begin to unveil and reveal themselves.

One by one, we will find Balance. And we will create a life that reflects that Balance and we will meet others who do the same. And we will create communities and we will prosper. It is happening even now.

And, you say, "What happens to those who choose imbalance, who choose to break the law of love, of Nature?" Then they shall experience what they create…until they learn from the pain of miscreations.

We need not teach them. Our lives are the message. If we are busy trying to interfere with their choices, how can we live the message?

Let us begin.
Let us follow the truth that sits so simply…
waiting in our hearts.

9-16-1997

Journey of Balance

The Law of Balance is the Law of Love. Sounds too simple, doesn't it? It is the inviolate law of the universe, without which the world would not exist. All would vanish. It is that which keeps all the known polarities in their dance of life. It is that which sends the rains to earth and then back to the heavens, only to reincarnate, by repeating the process again. It is the dance of the polarities in that realm which we know as Earth. We can observe for ourselves and see it in all of Nature's dance. Centripetal-centrifugal, compression-expansion, condensation-evaporation, hot-cold, masculine-feminine. On and on the list does go, for our own witnessing and beholding of the dance of Balance. That Balance plays itself out in equal giving and regiving. For Nature…it only gives. In giving…is the regiving. It is an inviolate and inexorable law.

I learned of this law from Law Russell in 1981. She was an exceptional woman who was born without the veils dropping. She was born remembering the law of balance which is the law of love. She spent her life in witness to this law. She described herself as a messenger from God to carry the message of love. She knew this was not a new message. She also knew that most messages get lost in adoration of the messenger. The message of Love is a very scientific message about this inviolate and inexorable law of balance demonstrated by all of Nature. The law of love is not about any messenger; it is about living and demonstrating love. Then we, too, become the messengers of love.

How is this law of balance, this law of love, this inviolate law of equal polarities, playing out in the kingdom of human life and in the man and woman realm? How is the balance of masculine-feminine polarity playing out in our own being and in the man-woman relationships in the created 3-D world? In the world home? In the work world? In the global home?

In a recent national address from the White House, it was stated that the goal of America for the next fifteen years was telecommunications, i.e., high tech world. That is the speaking of the masculine polarity world. This masculine display of high tech world by itself is out of balance. It can self-destruct. It is one polarity. It must be balanced by the feminine message of Essence of Life. It must address the feminine message of the true values of loving one another worldwide. It must address the imbalanced acts of polluting air, earth, water, and food with poisons and toxins. It must address the problems in the world with questions that truly bring solutions.

How is it…
that we may live the Law of Balance in this world?

How is it…
that we may live to have clean air, earth, water, and food?

Without the right questions, that high-tech telecommunications is still wide open to misuse. And history…it will repeat.

It is time. It is time we have balanced masculine and feminine messages in the community homes, as well as the world home. It is time we have the gifts of both…the masculine and feminine contributions. It is time that we have them in institutions everywhere…education, industry, politics, science, religion. It is time we fulfill this law of love/balance in all areas of our cultures, our lives, that the human kingdom may join finally in harmony with Nature, that already knows the law of balance and always gives.

The breaking of the law of balance brings imbalance. And we have free choice, so we may break the law. Thus wars, killing, lying, impoverished conditions, stealing, and on and on. But it is an inviolate law, this law of balance. And it will correct itself. Thus we hear the Eastern religions speak of karma, and in the Western ones we hear, "One reaps what one sows."

If the world would ask the right questions, we could begin a journey of never ending rapture, a journey of balance. We can ask ourselves how this alliance for balance can take place in our own world, in the man-woman world, in the local, national, and global transactions of giving and regiving.

It is at times almost difficult to remember, with this warring world, that there is a singular principle of love being enacted upon this little orb we know as Earth. And it is the dance of love. Love's dance upon this Earth. It is a spectacular and exquisite dance of the polarities. It is utterly simple in principle. So simple, as to be almost missed.

The residue and fallout and tension of imbalance takes most of the attention of humanity. It has been turned into a national and international attraction. It is watched in movies and videos and read in books everywhere. It is the modern coliseum of Rome. It is our entertainment. Our pastime. Talking about the disasters or preparing for the forthcoming disasters and tragedies and Armageddons. It is nonsense. It is all based on a lie. False premise. For it is based on imbalance which is the breaking of the law of the universe…love. We waste our time in vain. And we imagine that it is a wrathful god or that we are victims of Nature or empires and on.

> When will we get very simple…
> and together…remember there is only love?

When will we ask how can we love?

How can we individually and collectively
give love a body,
give love a form
upon this little spinning orb we know as Earth?

If every child in home and classroom was given the "problem" to solve, of how do they want to share their love, what a different world would come. Even the act of separating church and state. What folly to take love out of the demonstration of the governing of our countries and counties and cities! What folly to separate love from anything. How blind we are when we attack the problem, instead of asking the simple questions around fulfilling the law of love of this very precious universe in which we live.

Even now the new physicists are awakening and finding that there is a bigger force, though they give it scientific names. This knowledge is ancient...not new. Friends, there is a creator manifest as creation. A One come as the many. It is time to know for ourselves that Creator/Spirit is manifest as Creation/Nature. The One as the Many. We must each come to understand, know, experience, and realize ourselves as one with the minerals, plants, animals, and humans. That Oneness reveals the interconnectedness, the interrelatedness, the wholeness, the unity. Friends, we are One.

And much of humanity is playing like we are not. Those who see the vision of Oneness, who perceive the dance of balance, must become its messengers.

Messengers of Balance.
Messengers of love.

There is no other way…though we will express it in infinite forms…using endless names for this nameless One. Someone might ask how anyone could be so bold as to say, there is no other way. In our hearts and deep within our Soul, it is written. The Word. And it awaits. It awaits our departure from the world of imbalance and the sense of separation and pain. It awaits our return. It awaits all our journeys into psychic realms, into phenomenal realms, into outer space and into alien realms and on. It awaits. And it…is silent. And it knows.

You know. I know. Everyone knows. But we have not remembered. We must travel inward to remember. To know. To realize. We can know, direct within our hearts. Awaiting in our center is love, is balance. And that is the way.

How we enact that dance of love is myriad, is diverse, is ever changing, is the wonder of creator as creation. It is we who must open and allow that love to dance and sing and create and construct. And it will reflect the Wholeness of Balance.

There is only war and disharmony when humanity does not ask the right questions!

> How may we walk in balance?
> That is, how may we walk in love?
> No more bargains or getting the best deal!
> No more taking advantage!
> No more taking!

People are running about everywhere looking for love from somebody, sometimes almost anybody. Love is not a commodity. It is the Mystery. It is the Dance of Balance. It is something we find deep within our Being. It is something we give. We are that very love.

As we give, so we are given. Nothing new. Ancient. It is in many scriptures in some form. It is the law of the fulfillment of supply. And it is ancient. If we contain it, cage it, enclose it, crystallize it, freeze it…stopping its liquid flow…we find hate, enmity, growths in the body, boredom, anger, stagnation, no soul growth, almost no growth, fear. A seeming sense of separation from Source is a losing of contact with the love. And it breeds imbalance.

Although none of this is new, sometimes in our own fear orientation, we forget. And sometimes we need a reminder to go within to our own center to remember for ourselves. This is the only center that will ever give us the revelation of balance, of the inner marriage.

But we are so afraid. We call it stress or a hard day. We call it by many names. But its name is fear. Fear loses its life in the direct knowing of love. It disappears. It dissolves as if it never were. Love brings growth, and growth means change. We are even afraid of change, for that means loss of the familiar, the safe, the secure. So we begin to die in this safe, stagnant routine, in this controlled environment, which we ourselves created.

It is time to walk into the flow of life, the current of life which is the flow of love from within our Being. It is time to allow that flow of love to be as our "casting of bread upon the waters" and allow the regiving.

This is the journey of balance.

3-2-1997, in Mount Shasta, California

Animated by Infinity

Lao Russell, of the University of Science and Philosophy, studied civilizations down through the ages. She found that the measure of man-woman equality and balance in a civilization is the measure of the Love/Balance in that culture. In the enactment of balance and equality between man and woman are borne cultures that leave behind warring nations.

One need only to study or observe the divorce statistics to see that many human marriages are not working. Some people marry for lust, security, money, status, while others marry out of loneliness and desperation. Others are following social patterns, perhaps seen in advertising, movies, or homes. Still others may be escaping a situation. Whatever the reason, if it was not unconditional love, animated from the Infinite, it will not last. It may last in legal terms by staying married or in the same home. But it will not last.

It will not last because it never started.

Only unconditional love animated by Infinity is a lasting love.

We can, not only look deep within to find the unconditional love that we already are, but we can love all those about us. This essence…the Presence of love…it is everywhere present.

As we abide in that, we are a magnet for love relatings.

The SHE and HE coming together is a most natural fulfillment of the universal law. This law is the law of love, the law of balance, and it is inviolate.

Patriarchal Genocide

We are in for a change. A great change. The simple truth is that patriarchal society and patriarchal civilization does not work. Whether the form is within communism, socialism, tribalism, or democracy, it does not work.

A mind-energy dominated world does not work. Remember all one's history courses. And learning of all the wars. No matter what one names a patriarchal culture politically, it simply does not work.

We have witnessed and studied the patriarchy by many names and in cultures and civilizations through the ages. And they all war. From arrows and tomahawks to atomic and nuclear bombs, it is still war. It does not matter how many sacred ceremonies or prayers have been done, nor by whom. What is important is the life lived, the life demonstrated.

We are all looking for a wonderful and perfect model. It will not be found in patriarchy. It will not be found amongst the warring ones. It simply will not be found.

Where will we find that model? That template for Peace! We will find it in our Consciousness. In our inner Consciousness, where Balance does dwell. Where the inner marriage does dwell. It will then be found in outer Balance…in man-woman Balance. Woman, the life-giver, the protectress, must be part of the equation. Balanced and Equal. Reciprocity…it is the fulfillment of the inner law.

We approach a new day, a new Earth, and a new millennium. We have the opportunity to live it in Balance.

This is the opportunity to live the Law of Balance, in all of Nature. It is the only way we will be in harmony with Nature.

Or Nature, she shall spit in our face, as we smother in our own self-created pollution of earth, air, water, and food.

A culture of imbalance is as an errant child. It has lost half its Nature. It has shunned half its Nature. It has strangled and raped half its Nature. And it suffers greatly. The imbalanced patriarchal societies suffer greatly. They have suffered greatly through the ages. And they have created endless patriarchal structures of governments and control that allow little or no voice and little or no expression to the other half of our Nature. And that allow no change.

And yet, paradoxically, we are on the brink, the precipice of change. The Law of Balance in all of Nature fulfills that very law. The solutions are just waiting to be perceived by those who ask the simple question. How do we live in Balance with all of Nature? Heart and mind together. Harmony…it comes…

11-5-1997

Charmed

Each woman must move through "charmed"
to have her voice back...

Charmed keeps her voice damned.
Charmed keeps her in fear.
Charmed keeps her frozen.
Charmed damns the evolution of humanity.
Charmed seals the fate of woman
and locks tight the doors of her Self...her Soul...

Trembling does she take on the plight...
Trembling does she enter the doors of slave...
Trembling does she wear her baubles and smile anyway...
Trembling does she leave freedom borne of the Soul...
Trembling does she weave her own demise.

And now, as for eons of rising and falling civilizations,
does woman weep in her forlorn nights...

Now does she enter a darkness of her Soul
and ride the horse of despair...

Now does she feel only free to wiggle her hips
and serve that one who charmed her heart...

O woman...chose whom you shall serve this day...

She sits crying.
She sits crying for her lost Self.
She sits crying for her lost voice.
She is in the desert of her journey.

Her fate is sealed.
Charm has sealed her fate.
And death has come her way.
For her actions are not true.
Her voice is empty…
Her days are hell…
and her nights they have no end.

She does wonder where her life did escape…
As she sits in a cell called Charmed…
Days, weeks, months, and even years do pass…
and she sees that she is as a bird in a cage…
It is subtle…
Charmed is subtle…and clever…
Magic creates an unseen cage…
She is in it…before she knows…

No one threw her in. Or even pushed.
No…she danced in with eyes opened…blinded by the Charm.

O it is a blind spot in history, I say.
It is a blight…that knows no end…
Futility cooks the meals and pays the bills.
Jammed now are the circuits of He and She…
She has no voice…
And He has no truth…

He struts around armed with the sword of control.
Martial is no longer an art.
It has become the coat of arms
and women around the globe…
do curse the ancient day that woman
walked into the cage of charm
only to deposit their Soul in hell…

Not just the women of this day.
No…mothers, aunts, sisters, and grandmothers
running the course of history.
Woman knows this cage.
She did say yes.

Without a yes, he would leave…she thought.
He would find another she…
She would be alone…
She feared losing him…
She feared most everything…

Even has the social order been set up around Charmed.
O woman…now awake.
Awaken from your slumber and your spell.
Awaken from the lie.

This was not Prince Charming.
He was the demon from hell…
and he had hold of your heart…
your soul…
and even your body is his…

A slave you are in these times…

Awaken now from this sleep…
from this nightmare borne in time…

Call back your Voice…
Call back your Truth…
Find another Charm…

The Voice of Truth carries Beauty…
Anger and seething hatred do fall away…

Calm becomes the inner silent storm
that knows no end…
Calm becomes the volcano of emotions…
erupting as sorrow, sadness, and a despair that does not cease…

O woman…come out from this cage…
and call your sisters Home…

O woman…come out from your cage…
and find your sisters everywhere…
In villages and cities and nations…
around the globe…do they weep…

O woman…Beauty…rise up and speak your Truth…

Truth has no bad consequences.
Truth can only be the Bringer of Beauty…

O woman…this day…make another vow…
O woman…be a Bringer of Beauty…

For Beauty-SHE does bring the Balance…
Beauty-SHE is the bringer of True Charm…
And Charm…shall lead the way…

O woman…the world does wait in tears for you…
The world does need a Mother…
And SHE must be the Bringer of Balance…

SHE must dance as the goddess of reciprocity.

SHE must arrive empty to do this Dance…
A glowing current shall enter and dance…
And freedom it shall come…

And it shall flower over the land...
Time shall cease...

Enter on the stage of Life...Beauty HE and SHE...
And Charm shall flow across the lands and across the seas...
And fairy tales are true...

2-4-2004, 6 a.m.

Why has SHE allowed?

Woman does not allow a dirty home...
She cleans, She washes, She scrubs...

Why has woman allowed a dirty world-home?

Why has she been silent?
Why has she allowed dirty air?
Why has she allowed dirty water?
Why has she allowed chemicals in her foods?
Why has she allowed genetic alterations?
Why has she allowed pesticides in the earth?
Why has she allowed?
Why has she allowed the earth to stink...
to blow abominations from stacks...
from cars...from engines everywhere?
Why has woman allowed this filth?
Why has woman shut her eyes or looked the other way?
Why has woman allowed the harming of the children?
Why has woman allowed the suffering of the animals
in endless industries?

Books have been written on the environment, our world-home...
and on the animals, our brothers and our sisters...
And still we remain silent...

Where is the Mother of the World?
Where has she gone?

We don't need endless statistics to prove these words.
We need only to go within the heart to know...
go within the soul...

What will one's answer be when we are told…
It is impure…

The answer is simple…
The answer has always been simple…

Let us cast our votes…
Let us cast our votes for a clean and non-suffering world…

It is simple…

The Mother of the World lives within your heart.
She knows.

Find her and she will live beneath your breasts
and beat within your heart…
and act within this world…

2-26-2005, mid-day in Taos, New Mexico

Law of Balance...

We have had nothing but rising and falling civilizations, that have not been civilized, throughout history. Perhaps we might look at Nature and learn her simple Law of Balance. She gives and is regiven. Simple.

That is the law of balance. That is the law of love. It is inviolate and inexorable. We break it and it will break us. Simple.

Civilizations have not learned. The bully in the block becomes the empire builder and/or politician and gets money and human power to lord over others in insidious ways. Taking...always taking. This will not change until we understand, live, and demonstrate the Law of Balance. Simple.

There will be no "we, the people" until we understand the Law of Balance. In the homes, we need a mother and a father. Balanced and equal. In all of the governing bodies of Earth...at home, local, county, state, national, and international levels... we need balance and equilibrium. We will have that when we have the governing by equal men and women. The Mother of the Home is understood. Now we must understand the Mother of the World. The world needs a mother/mothers. The feminine point of view, as a balancing force in the civilizations, has been missing. Until man and woman are equally governing the nations, we will not have enduring cultures. President/Presidenta, King/Queen, and on...

It is of utmost clarity that men, alone, cannot govern a civilization. His-story itself has spoken. That revelation is not spoken, but it is known. Wars and battles and never-ending materialism are valued. The feminine part of our nature desires to express love, equality, appreciation, relationship, deep communing, balance, respect, and honoring. That must become an integral part of our governing bodies, everywhere, at every level of government, including homes and nations.

People use adages like, we can only have freedom via "blood, sweat, and tears." Perhaps that is so when one is speaking of human freedom "from." Freedom from oppression, suppression, depression. Pressure and authority from the outside.

There is another freedom, friends. It is "freedom in." Freedom in a Presence, that is a universal presence, that religions, traditions, and groups throughout history have named and fought about. Crusades, inquisitions, and on. Until we individually and then collectively come to "realize" that Presence is Presence, by whatever name, we shall continue, yes, the "blood, sweat, and tears." It is a path we need not take.

Any individual, group, or nation that turns to this Presence will find itself being guided and even lived…by this Presence. It is up to us. We can live by free will or by this Presence that moves the very stars. It is our choice. This Presence knows no opposition, no battle, no war. Ever. It is the oneness of all creation. It works together in harmony. We can be with it or against it. Simple.

Should we choose to believe in freedom, via "blood, sweat, and tears," we begin with a false premise. We must all be wary of false premises. They can be dressed up and disguised easily via intellectualism and ignorance. Then we live in the masquerade and join the world in pain, suffering, and misery borne of imbalance. Instead, we must ask to know the universal principle.

The universal principles are laws of Nature, which are laws of balance. Laws of love…that give in order to be regiven. Simple.

The civilizations that have risen and fallen have lived lives of taking. The form of that taking has created endless horrors for humanity and Nature. And it will end when we decide it will end.

All the knowledge and repeating and memorizing of his-story has not stopped the wars and battles…ever. Here and there, we have unspeakable examples in front of us, but we fail to see the implication. Gandhi, each night, went within, and received guidance. That is how he succeeded in creating freedom for millions. It was "freedom in" the withinness, the Presence, that guided him. He was not battling, warring, or fighting… or reacting.

Gandhi lived a rare life, responding to the inner vision, rather than reacting to the world of human concepts and the outer battle borne of imbalance.

We must ask the question of ourselves. How can we live an exemplary life? How can we "respond to the inner Vision" and act in the world, rather than react and fight in the world? There is a great difference here. Reaction acknowledges the problem and perpetuates it in the battle.

We hear constantly throughout his-story of the haves and have-nots. We continue to battle, and finally the have-nots "win" and the haves become the have-nots. They exchange roles when one finally usurps the power over the other. Always through taking. This life of endless battle of the haves and have-nots will not end collectively until there is an understanding of the universal principle of Consciousness about having and not having.

Having and not having is a "state of consciousness." Those who attain a strong enough having consciousness will "have," even if they have to steal, plunder, rape, or kill. Those who believe they have-not will also get their due, which is their belief. When we begin to understand the Law of Balance, which is giving to be regiven, then this sick and painful and untrue period of history will end. It will come one person at a time. All can be prosperous. All can have. We must be willing to learn the Laws of Nature and teach them to our children. We must be willing to be the living demonstration of this universal principle of supply. We need not continue to seek throughout the eons of ways to "redistribute the wealth." Wealth and supply just are, and we see it not. We have been so busy "taking." We have been so busy fighting, believing the false premise that we must fight to "have." Let us go to Nature. An apple tree does not need to take apples from other trees to have supply. The examples are endless.

Let us become individuals, families, and nations that give!
Let us together live the Law of Balance.
Let us ask what that would look like!
Let us begin this day!

Democracy needs a new face.
All the governing bodies of the world need a new face.
That face is woman. Mother of the World.

The world needs a mother.
We need to have a balance...
Mother and Father of the World...
and the imbalance...it will end...

We, ourselves, have created this immense imbalance
down through the eons.

The Voice of the Feminine,
through woman, needs to be heard.
And balance...it will come...

This is not a matter of the ridiculous fight for "woman's rights." Woman, everywhere, must ask within, how can I contribute to the actual living of this inviolate Law of Balance? Woman must just "live it." This is not a pitiful pleading for equality. Woman is Already equal. She just has failed to ask within HOW to live it. And men, everywhere, will begin to see that this Law of Nature has been broken through the ages. And those who begin to see will begin to find unspeakable and unprecedented ways to live this Law of Balance.

A new world; it does emerge.

What has been missing from the world is Man/Woman Balance. It is time that women and men everywhere take the responsibility to go within and find their own unique way of demonstrating balance. The only true Power is in the Law of Balance. Everything else is a breaking of the natural law and has in it the seeds of destruction that cause the falling of a civilization.

It is time that the world see that this has absolutely nothing to do with "fighting for woman's rights." It is simply a matter of going within and finding "HOW to live as Already balanced and equal." The world of imbalance will begin to crumble and dissolve if we, ourselves, are not there giving it power…via fear, battle, reaction, and endless other bits of inappropriate attention.

We can begin to add her-story to his-story to have a True-Story! Man/woman balance upon this little spinning orb we know as Earth…finally dancing with the law of balance in all of Nature…

Vision…
just live the Vision…

2004

Honor Nature Now

Our present culture will be remembered in the future as barbaric. Barbaric and savage. We who remove animals from their Nature. We who carry them from their habitats. We who place them in cages. We who cause them long pain and suffering, out of Nature, away from their own kind.

Who are we? Out of our own True Nature, we have become the fiends to Nature. We have become those who tear trees from the ground, tear the children from play, tear adults from their dreams.

Fiends to Nature we have become. And liars of the grandest sort. "Say no to drugs" we tell our children, as we fill our medicine cabinets, bodies, and foods and drinks and soil with chemicals of the grossest sort. And we wonder that we are a disease-ridden nation. We have pillaged Nature…and she does know.

What we have not reckoned with is that Nature has the last word. Nature is the reaction to our actions. And she is starting to speak. We need to be listening. All the warnings are with us now.

Nature is the law unto Balance. And should we break the inviolate Law of Balance, it is we who pay the price. We pay the price for breaking this universal Law of Nature. And we then pretend Nature is bad. Weather is bad. Or even worse, that some faraway God is doing it. We…we are doing it, my friends. And we are reaping what we sow. And we are living the reactions to our very own actions.

We need to "ask to know." We need to desire to know. Know

how to live in Balance, in harmony with all of Nature. We need to let the animals go. Zoos everywhere will close and we shall know a better day.

Let us put our minds to better use. Smogless cars and smogless industry. What? We can get a man to the moon, but not have smogless cars. We can have global telecommunications and not have clean air, water, earth, and food. We are a living farce. Our culture is a farce.

How long will we, the people, give our responsibility away in this culture? How long and far will we stray from Nature before the pain is too great?

>How loud must Nature roar?
>How great must be the waves?
>How many birds in the sky must die?
>How great must be the pain?
>
>We are standing on the brink.
>We are poised…
>about to begin a new day or lose our natural way…
>
>Let us join the Force of Nature…
>playing a part in Nature's Play…
>Let us honor Nature now!

The audacity to build a culture that doesn't honor Nature…

How dare we hand such disrespect of Nature to our children…
>How dare we plunder Nature's resources for a coin…
>How dare we forget to value Nature…
>How dare we forget to value Balance…

And now does the Mother raise her head…
and her body…to speak…
and slay if necessary…
She is ready to react to our actions.
And thus begin a new day.

We need to be Present to change our ways…
We need to pay homage to the Mother…

Let us honor Nature now…

4-28-1997, after morning meditation in Mount Shasta

Temple of Darkness

My child, sexuality has been known as the scourge of the ages, all because church and state wanted to control the people, man and woman. It is a very time-tested way in which it has been done. Divide and conquer. If man could be made to believe that woman and/or sex was somehow wrong or even evil, the goal of divide and conquer had been accomplished. And with that came the battle of the ages.

Woman has not only fought for her rights, she has only her own dim recollection of what sexuality really is. She knows that in her own moist temple of darkness lies a something which she cannot quite define. And so it is, that she lures man into this "temple of remembering."

Unless man and woman are in the Infinite, they will not experience the Treasure of this Temple. Nor will they couple as guided by the Life that courses through their veins. Instead they shall be attracted for social, mental, financial, and physical reasons. They will pass through the nights, grasping and gasping for a something that ever eludes.

> The world awakens from a lie told long ago.
> The world awakens from the pain
> of never finding the outer one,
> for they never found the Inner One.
>
> The world has been in the anguish of the fog of the lie…
> while even the butterflies of the field
> do find their mates for life…
> and yet…humans insult the insect world…

Never has the time been so ripe as now.
There is an invisible matrix in place.
It is an illumined matrix of joined consciousness…
It shall either create harmony or havoc in one's life…
Static shall cease to be.

Man and woman…they shall change…
Separations of misguided relatings shall occur.
Illumined knowing shall pour across the lands…
The fog of unknowing shall lift…
The Mystery of the Ages…shall dance…
Man and woman shall dance as One…

No longer shall the lies be the bringers of human misery…

No longer shall men secret a rape…
or long for the empty shell of lust…

No longer shall woman weep at night,
for she knows not what…
nor shall she tremble at unfulfilled longing…

Yes…it is true…the Beloved is within…
Yes…it is true…the mystical marriage is within…
And…it is true…that in that realization that
the inner is known as the outer…

The boundaries cease to be…
The inner One…is the outer one…

1-12-2003, while driving to San Francisco
(words of Isis that came to me)

foresee the Day of Venus

O woman…you have waited patiently
through the ages and the eons…
Hoping, yearning for man to see
the wings you use to touch the heaven world…
You have begged, connived, cajoled…
hoping he would see your feathers borne of light…
You have disgraced yourself
by forgetting the Soul that is your lord…

O woman…come…rise…
Rise now…finally after millenniums of moons…
Rise and be the woman that you are…
Rise and be the woman…the mother of the world…

O woman…there is no return…
only in the filth of rape…
only in the cage with locks…
only in the harem of surface lust…
only in the maid of servitude…
does lie your tomorrows in your return…

O woman…use your wings…
Fly to the heaven world…
and find your dance…

I say…find your dance…
find your dance…
that man may notice…
that man may observe…
that man may support…
that man may conjoin…

It is that time, I say, on the calendars of your time…

Arise…take flight…
Woman…in the annals of time…
is only preparing to be known…

And only when she is known…
will man be known…

For woman does fuse this world with the heaven world…
Woman does rend the veil
and give glimpses of the morning star…
Woman does walk the form and formless as one path…

O SHE does wear the secret of eternity in her heart…

O woman…hear the call of that secret of eternity…
Foresee the day of Venus…
Glimpse that world and dance…
In your heart…is the savior you so longed for…
in the outer world…

I tell you…woman…
You must do the dance…
and now the time grows short…

11-12-2004, while driving through the canyon to Santa Fe

Illumined Creature of the Sea

Mary, dear one, we are here. We have long awaited this day. You began to open to your own starry memories of us in the mid to late eighties. During your sickness/nausea, you felt a need to just do what it took to stay alive. Strong you grew during this period. Your desire to move to an island in 1988. That was us. Prompting you always to spend much solitary time in Nature. And that, dear child, is what you did in every free moment. You have thought you were not listening well enough. You are right on time. We are here now. You have never wanted there to be a "we" speaking to you. You have always wanted just the singular God Presence. We are that.

We carry now, yet another message be to given to the children of Earth at this time. It is a message that will crack open, yet another layer of the concepts that hold the collective back from the rapture that does await.

If you lose "contact," just breathe and merge into the field of love as you do when you meditate and as you go about your day.

You have long wished, my child, that you came in a different body. You have seen the easy lives of women in other bodies, as they are grabbed up by the men. You, child, chose your current body, petite and very slight, for a specific purpose. You did not want to fall into the trap of being defined externally. You came with strong intention to break those earthly ties, so crusted in concepts and human limitation. You chose this body, that you might wax strong in your identity as spirit. You longed to stay connected and assist in this time of remembering Oneness.

We have come strongly to you for many years. Now we come to

deliver more understanding to those of the Earth for this time of rapid change and transformation.

We want to speak through you of many things. Let us begin with the subject that is so misunderstood by the children of Earth: Man and Woman...

Child, the relationships of man and women look nothing like what will come to pass in what you know as future. As concepts break and crumble and dissolve and fall away from the human mind, the women of your species will lead a shift in the nature of the relationships. She, who is the lover of beauty and harmony of every step, she shall redefine the world. She awakens rapidly now to the dance of the Infinite. This dance does gain momentum. There is no stopping the surge of this dance, as it breaks through into her consciousness, guiding her dance.

Woman appears to be the stronger gender spiritually, for the heart does guide the way. As this dance grows within her heart, there is no looking back. Woman shall not look back into the annals of history that is a living lie. She shall ride the crest of this wave as an illumined creature of the sea, as a goddess stepping forth from archetypal realms, not to be studied, but to Cause the change. Woman is deeply connected to Cause.

The missing piece from history's volumes shall step forth and do her Dance. And history shall change. And history shall end.

Ones shall begin to drop the routines from their lives. They shall drop the schedules of times past. They shall inherit instead inner inklings that shall appear as their day. Days shall come and go. These routines and schedules are as veils that are worn as blinders to the Beloved.

Another Beloved does enter the field.

The men shall gasp as woman finds delight in the Beloved everywhere. The spell of sex…it shall be broken. Women everywhere shall know that their delight is in all things.

The world shall enter a new era. Woman, the goddess, as independent of man. This independence is not just financially, but emotionally and in all ways.

In this freedom, there is no choice for man to do anything but change. For woman will have created a new dynamic. Woman will have offered a new configuration.

There is no history here. There are no books to read. There are no books written by men for men to define woman. The old texts are dead. It has already happened. Women around the world feel it and are saying yes. The yes is a response that lives in the heart. Ever are the ancient manuals that would posture a women…as dead.

A freedom, unprecedented, is hurtling through woman. Her voice is about to be heard around the world. It will be heard everywhere. In homes, in offices, in governments of the world. Woman shall have her day…and it is come.

> History shall no longer stifle this voice.
> The unheard voice…now heard.
> This voice…of the Infinite…now heard.

> Woman shall begin to gather like no other time.
> She will not gather in ways of the past.
> She shall gather to reflect the One.
> She is a force that cannot be stopped.

No longer shall the goddess be thought of as from history's lore or from mythology's worn pages or from some distant realms. She shall present herself as that. Living, breathing, birthing still. No need to drag out the books to read of the goddess. She shall surface everywhere. Inside each home shall she appear. Beside each child shall she walk.

No longer…
shall the goddess send the babies of her womb to war.

No longer,,,…
will she sanction toxins or buy them in the store.

No longer…
will she pay the price for impure water
and the dying of the species.

The mother arises. She is felt through all women. Many will be perplexed when the thoughts begin to come to her. She will ponder, be perplexed, and then she will perceive.

She will perceive the path of death and destruction.

She will perceive the course that humanity takes in the spell of the lies cast by history.

She will choose another way. She shall cast off the lies, like the casting off of demons. She shall create another path. This is a path that has no name. This is a path that appears, illumined, as she takes each step. This is a path that takes the knowing of the heart. There are no instruction manuals; there are no priests or outer teachers to point the way, keeping one a child.

Another world does birth that is not confined to text and teacher.

This world is not seen by our eyes. It is known in the heart and lived, just as a sculpture or a song does come to life. Out of nothing does it appear. From the formless does it come to form.

Woman shall lead the way.

Long has this been ignored.
The day has come.

Word shall travel from woman to woman.
Each will listen in their hearts.
And culture, true culture, shall finally borne.

Long has humanity awaited this time.
The time has come.

All of society shall restructure itself
as woman gives form to her heart.

Habits shall falter.
Destruction shall give way to beauty.
Fear shall give way to love.

Hearts everywhere shall sing…
Complex shall give way to simple…
Frowns shall end and endless smiles begin…

Rapture…it shall clothe the goddess…
Psychology shall be no more…
Truth shall reign…

Truth shall wear the crown of long ago
and travel through the mind of all…

Lies will be laughed at…
Deceit will be seen…
And corruption shall have no name…

O for eons woman has been silent.
Not silent from ignorance.
Nor silent from not knowing.
Woman has been silenced by fear.

Fear no longer dominates the goddess.
She has seen it dwells not in the heart.
She has seen another world.
Stunned by its beauty, she lives in another world.

Woman, it is, that knows that days of enslavement are done.
Those days are done for her.
They are done for the animals.

Cages are death.
Hideous it has been and it is done.
Few are the days left for its display of limitation.

Cages exist not in the heart…
Only freedom to be…

And Peace.
Peace is found only in the heart.
It is not found in battles and victories
and nations killing nations.
Peace is lived…not fought for.
Peace is not bargained for or bought or sold.
Peace is an outpouring from within.
Peace is felt when fear does flee.
Peace lives in a heart of love.

And woman, she does know.
She knows it in simple ways…
suckling her child…
and even the child does know…

O warriors of the world. There is no battle.
And woman…she does know.
She has remained silent for an age or so…
and now the words do come…

Woman's hand shall open now new doors.
Doors beyond traditions and times past.

Procedures and processes of the mind…
they shall fall away…

Mary, child, we know that you fear that this is "gender" talk. We know that you would prefer to not be letting this through. Stay open to Presence and we shall guide you through this block. What you open in yourself is available to all. You wrote "She…it is…who Remembers" in '87–'88. Now is the time for the collective movement of woman to break forth. It will be an unforeseen "global movement" of great proportions. Listen within. Observe without.

2-12-2005

Worth Endless Eternities...

I long to tell my sisters…that which cannot be told…
I long to say…you look…you walk…in the wrong direction…
I long to say…look into the vast…withinness…
and HE…is there…
I tell you…HE…is there…

Some tell me…they don't care…
Some tell me…it's not worth the wait…
Woman…I tell you…it is…
It is worth endless eternities…
endless births and deaths…
It is worth it all…
I tell you…it is…

I can gather with you…sing and dance…
I can tell you stories of the secret entrance…
I can lead you up many paths…

But I cannot walk you in…
No one can walk you in…
It is not even a walk…
On the other side of the sheer burning pain…
borne of two powers…
lies a secret entrance…

It awaits you…
It awaits me…
It awaits us all…
Let us enter now…

1-15-2003, while driving to Seattle

O Woman…Ask to Know…

O woman…fair and beautiful woman…
Can you hear when your sister speaks…the unspeakable?
When she speaks of union of HE and SHE…can you hear?
Is your pain of not having…too great to hear?
Is your pain of not having…too great to know?
What would you give to know?
What would you give up…to know?

O woman…ask to know!
Or Greatness…you shall never meet…
It shall be as a stranger on the darkest night…
Always cloaked…always secreted away…

O woman…treasure you…the women who walk ahead…
Treasure those who open doors to the Vastness…
Leave coveting…as if it never were…
for woman…also…this Vastness…it is yours…

1-15-2003, while driving to Seattle

Wordless Songs to the Moon

Somewhere…anywhere…
is there someone with whom I may speak…
To whom may I share…that which has no words…
And what may I share…when all words cease to be…
Shall I dance alone in the night to the Infinite?
Shall I sing wordless songs to the moon…
with wolf howling as my primal-He?
Will this song of songs be heard?
Or shall it go unnoticed…
in the world where tears flood away the joy…that Is…

1-15-2003, while driving to Seattle

Cauldron of Creator: Amriti of He and She

I am awakening at an accelerated rate to the profound, holy, and sacred role of man and woman. They are a paradox…outer man and woman. They are the yin-yang symbol.

They are the black and the white, the chalice and the blade, the feminine and masculine. Yet they are neither. They are One. They form the perfect balance, the perfect template for the dance of the One.

>They are ever in the Cauldron of Creator.
>They are ever the alchemical union of the divine.
>They are ever harmony manifest.

With this Balance as the cradle of a society…only Beauty will grow. Cultures of unprecedented Beauty shall arise out of the humus of ashes and decay. Only Beauty can survive this cradle.

Searching in the annals of history's pathology will never build a culture. In those annals lives only the fear, suffering, and pain borne of imbalance. In those annals lives the records of rising and falling civilizations fed on the fascination of pathology.

Humanity has a new hunger. That hunger is fed each time a woman covers her body in a way that reveals her Soul Beauty… and it shines forth and radiates in her physical body, gestures and postures.

>Truly Beauty comes.
>SHE comes.
>And SHE comes undaunted.

SHE wears a sword at her hip.
SHE is a wild dakini free of tradition.
SHE soars to the highest stars
and plunges to the deepest bowels…
SHE is wild…raw…primal…primordial
in the writhing and turning…
SHE…is the child of Union…

Under starched collars of priests
does live the steamy sweat of sex…
does live the truth that union is a template of holiness…

Sex invokes the invisible template of holiness.
This template is a key.
It is a key to the building of the new cosmology.
It can't be staged or faked or bought or sold.
It can't even be hoped for…pushing it as a carrot
ever into the non-arriving future…
It can be acknowledged…as Is…
Already Is…
And then does come…a magnetism of perfect balance…
It is the alchemy that already exists…
We can be one with this and allow…

Allow the unseen to be seen…
the unheard to be heard…
Allow the mystery to dance naked…

Allow the union of He and She…to unveil itself…
Allow the veils to flow…
the smile to come…
Allow the chalice to be filled
in the womb and in the crown…
Allow heaven's doors to open wide…

Allow Beauty's story to be seen and heard
and danced upon the earth…

Without change…
some traditions may hear the death rattle…
All the techniques in the world
will never create Amriti of He and She…

Locked away have remained the secrets…
So hidden has been the knowledge
that Union has been dressed in slime…
and degraded and denigrated almost beyond recognition…
Union has been abased and shattered…
It has become the nemesis…
rather than the key…
It is too often used as a relief
from a world that does not know…
It is used as a last gasp of hope
for a moment of pleasure…

It stands unseen…
as an ultimate spiritual practice…
It lies hidden in its mysteries…

It stands all too often utterly vulgar and profane…

It stands unseen…waiting…
unprecedented power and force
to be unleashed upon this earth…

The cult (gathering) of Isis…
it arises…
There is no club to join…
It is found only in the darkest recesses of withinness…

It is found in the inner alchemy of the wedding…
the yin/yang union
of inner lover and beloved.

Only that can create the alchemy of the outer union…
and only then…when both are in full readiness…
And they do change the world…
Through them sacred geometries
do synapse in the brain…
Through them earth and sky do meet…
and dusk and dawn…
and
borne
is
Beauty…

Beauty borne of the union of wisdom and love…
He and She…day and night…
Beauty borne of unbridled passion
scorching all those minds
that would call for chastity…
Chastity is called in…only for unholy unions…

It draws near…
Holy Union…
It draws near…

Traditions shall be exposed…
not just Enrons and Halliburtons
but sons of the most ancient of structures
that would keep the lid on the truth…
that yin and yang must be kept separate…

How subtle has been the cloaking of
the Power of the Infinity by man…

How subtle and how insidious does this structure rule...
How truly impotent man has become in its grasp
using a tool to become powerful
that strikes him powerless.

Even now...the veils of Beauty thin...
her Beauty stands naked
and undisguised...

More words do not serve...
This is an Initiation of Direct Revelation...
It can only be found on the inner space
of Holy Union...

Vamp, seductress. slut, and whore...
She has been given many names...
No one has taken Her seriously
for even She did not know
that She holds such mysteries
and that together...
HE and SHE may open finally the doors...

O woman...
May now you see...
May now you see the treasure...
the sought for eden and paradise...
the sought for nirvana and satori...

Why do it alone...
when we are the He and She of Creation...
within and without...

And woman shall not find it...
in a gilded dress...
or in the swaying of the jewel...within her hips...

No wonder at the restlessness in humanity…
No wonder something always feels incomplete…
And teachers…they can guide the way…
but they…they are not the It…

No wonder awakening woman was burned at the stake
and such…
She is the ever appearing reminder
of what lies waiting behind the veils…

Not only was woman's vote and equality taken from her
but the Power of the mystery she contains
was taken…
And it has been a sad history.

Where are the King and Queen of Heaven?
Where are they?
Finding Presence within and without…
as everywhere present…
is the beginning
of the unveiling
of an unprecedented world…
to behold and live…

Woman shall need to be fierce and dedicated
to open wide these doors…
These doors are an Initiation…
They are fires…
There is no turning back…

I ask the question…
Is woman a record keeper of the mysteries?

And I hear people talk of tantra…

If the traditional structure of tantra
has unearthed the mysteries…
why have millennia passed
and still yin/yang are not equal
across the lands and across the seas…

Clearly…the Mystery is not unveiled…

Let us not confuse promiscuity for sacred union…
Let us not confuse lust for sacred union…
Let us not confuse harem consciousness for sacred union…

Organizations, religions, traditions…
None of these are large enough to contain this direct revelation.
No structure may contain this direct revelation…

All that would contain…limits…
And there are no limits here…
All that would contain…controls…

It is time for an inner arising…
It is time for flights into Oneness
both within and without…

the winged serpent comes…
be certain of this…
the call has been sounded…
some do already hear…

12-11-2002

A King without a Queen?

Friends…
Is there a king without a queen?
Is there a prince without a princess?
And is there a shaman without a shamaness
or a priest without a priestess?
Is there a seer without a seeress or a husband without a wife?
Is there a yin without a yang or a mountain without a valley?
Is there an up without a down or is there a fast without a slow?

Friends…
We are that very dance of yin and yang.
We are that very dance within and without.
We are the very dance of the One as the Two.

Friends…
Is there centripetal without centrifugal?
Does a screw work without a hole?

The dance of the ages is that!
The dance of the polarities in unison.
The dance of the polarities in all of Nature.
The dance of the polarities as an outpouring of the One.

Friends…
it is a dance of love.
In man and woman,
in all of Nature,
there is only this dance.
First within.
Then without.

Let us reclaim that dance.
It is a dance of balance.
It is free and unencumbered.
It exudes rapture.
It is the tea ceremony that never ends.
It is the land of a vast epiphany.
Let it be…

9-26-2003, while driving from Taos to Santa Fe

Invitation to Intimacy

Intimacy can only be known by man and woman who are real, authentic, being moved from a silent force within. Both man and woman allowing of the birthing of themselves in each moment. And a full allowing of the other Self.

Only then…can depths be plunged.
Only then…can the miracle…the mystery of…
true intimacy occur.

True intimacy is a bonding borne of spirit…
not of human notions and controls…
True intimacy…conceives a child…
that child…a purpose from the fiery worlds…
True intimacy cannot be spoken…
it is a breath in time…and yet it leaves one breathless.
True intimacy is unutterable…the mind…
it is insane with no logic and reason…

O friends…invite intimacy…

It is not a study…
It is Being…
It risks everything…for it is borne of truth…
It is borne…for joy…
for joy of union…it is borne…
It is not a class…

One cannot plan or prescribe intimacy…
It is borne in the moment…
Exquisite union of the minds…
A precious intercourse of two minds…
Bodies joined is an effect…

O friends...
We are not our bodies...
Two stars do fly across the sky...
and they do join in the night...

Intimacy is unspeakable...
It stretches the mind to its farthest point...
and there...
mind dissolves...

There find...a holy entrance...
There find...another world...
There find...a new world...

O friends...it is this for which we search...

In this union...do we find the One...
In this world...is the awareness of One...
We are One...

I tremble...
I shake...
I shudder...
in the vast remembering...
Yes...it is good...

Invite intimacy...

1-15-2003, while traveling to San Francisco

Woman as Ransom

Over and over and over again...
man has made woman the ransom...
He hates pitiful woman, yet he makes her pitiful...
He loves swooning woman, so he can look strong...
playing ever the warrior with gun or sword...
playing ever the victor while the victim is she...
as the angel with broken wings...

Woman...arise...
Arise...and fly...

11-12-2004, while driving to Santa Fe

Liberation of Love

What occurs now on this globe is liberation of love…
It has been contained by lies.
It has been imprisoned.

You, my child, are one of the pioneers of this movement
of the liberation of love between man and woman.
You, my child, shall herald the partners in purpose.
You shall declare…
the coming of the new world…
that shall come two by two…
Child…carry this message to the people…

Even women gatherings…they shall change.

Women use woman circles to gather in the support, love, and appreciation not found in the coupling. Woman circles have a much loftier purpose. Together they anchor in the feminine principle. They strengthen that polarity.

And then…Balance…it can come…
The women…linked with the Infinite…in a Circle…
and it is done…

1-12-2003, while driving to San Francisco
(message from Isis)

Inner Sanctum of True Man and True Woman

There is a book that is highly read in the mainstream world that is regarded as a conscious book for all to read with information of what men and women are like and how they should act and respond to one another. If one has the motivation and a great memory, one can memorize "pat answers given to you" through another person, in this case the author. And then if one is sufficiently closed to the Infinity's flow, one can remember and recite the "pat answer" for the given situation.

Friends, how sad that we are so cut off, so separated from the Infinite that may flow through our minds, when we open to It, that we must resort to "pat answers" that are actually fully dead to the moment that we are in. Each moment is fresh and new and alive and has a response that is magical in the moment. That response, when from the Infinite, is a key that opens understanding, love, and beauty.

It may be a response never ever used again in a similar or any situation.

How far away have we strayed from our "own knowing and response." How far away have we strayed from Truth pouring through us. So how far away are we from True Man and True Woman?

How sad it is that we follow others' formulas, dictums. opinions, and theories.

How sad that we do not want to know for ourselves.

How sad that we have not yet found the inner sanctum of our being, where "knowing" pours forth.

Together…let us turn this plight around…
Together…let us know…
Together…let us find the harmony that Already IS…

9-26-2003, while driving from Taos to Santa Fe

Safe to Speak

I have the awareness that I have not incarnated fully because I learned from infancy that it is not safe to be here. You are not liked if you say your truth.

I have the awareness that many women have not incarnated fully, as it is not safe. They either become wimpy, weak-willed, and helpless women or they become like a man.

It is time for True Woman to emerge. Those two choices no longer work.

> And we might inquire, what is True Woman?
> How may she emerge?
> How may I, as woman, emerge?

9-7-2003, on a trip from Taos to Los Angeles

Illness: A Call for Change

Illness is a Call…a call for change. A change in diet or attitude or a change in beliefs. A change of job or residence or geography. A change of appearance or relationships or values or emotions. A change in quality of life, in quality of friends. Or perhaps a change in purpose.

Illness is a Call…a call for change in body and/or mind. Illness is a beacon of alert. A red light. Stop. Reevaluate your life in all ways. Take time to deeply touch the Spirit of your Being, that it may reveal the changes needed for body and mind.

Much of the human resistance to taking full responsibility for illness is the human resistance to change. Change means facing the unknown, the mystery. It may mean changing our lifestyle, our present habits, our addictions. It may mean facing ourselves. It may mean leaving our familiar career or our known routines.

It is a Call. A strong Call. Mind, Body, Spirit are not at One. At this point we need to ask the right question. If we limit our question to how can I fix the symptom in the effects world, we have placed great limitation on our great opportunity to shift, to change, to grow, to be in balance and Oneness with Creator and Creation.

This so-called illness is a warning of moving into imbalance. It is our clue that something is wrong. Something must change in our life.

So illness and imbalance become a Call for Change of Consciousness! We usually say, "I don't know what is wrong." So, in that, we pull the "veil of unknowing" over our Consciousness and feel we have a right to act like we do not know. We have created our own barrier to knowing. Only those who "ask to know" will begin to get the insights and glimpses of "knowing" what to change.

That "knowing" is in our own Consciousness. Our own Being. As we begin to "unveil," we begin to envision another life, a life that has been covered with fear...fear of change. This Life is ever moving, ever changing, ever filled with joy. And this Life is gifted from the unchanging One, the nameless One.

3-30-1997 Easter, in Mount Shasta, California

Monsters in Our Midst No More...

At our core we are all the same...
At the surface we are not...

For daily choices we have made
and carved our lives our way...

Our way brings us troubles
and rots our very lives...

Ones turn into monsters
and play with other lives...

They hurt the young; they maim the lives; they test the animals...

They test and torture and take no heed
to the sadness and the pain...

They turn their hearts to suffering
and pretend it is not there...

What has brought these monsters in our midst,
who behind closed doors would bring such pain?

Let us look up close...
These monsters...they are afraid...
They have been hurt and they are in pain...
They fear no funds...
They fear no supply...
so concessions they do make...

They fear no fame
and they are public saviors
wearing white lab coats…
scientists of our time…
out to find the next new test
that will save the public lives…

To find that fame and get that fund…
their hearts turn into stone…
White robed monsters in our midst…
have hearts that turned to stone…

They lost their feelings…
They lost their way…
Their hearts, they have no life…
They kill, they maim, they travel on…
to this darkness they made of pain…

Inflicting pain is indeed the game
and with it they have no gain…
They have no gain and the conflict grows…
for they seek name, through funds and fame…
This monster slowly grows
till finally feelings borne in the heart
are buried deep within…

Feelings buried so deep…
as if they have never been…
The monster is free now…
hideous life to live…

So how do we have
such monsters in our midst?

What form of greatness
do we bestow on these white robed ones!
Mad scientists in their labs...
assuring animals of tortured lives...

What form of gifts do we give these minds
who are monsters in our midst?

How is our culture the creators of this pain...
that hides in labs behind closed doors
with corporate grants for animal pain?

Pain that would make you sick...
Pain that would disgust...
Pain that would make you squirm...
Pain that would make you cry...

Pain that if you knew of its truth
would bring from you a wail...
A wail so deep, so filled with pain...
an anguish beyond the known...

And as others know, the wail would grow...
the masses...they would wail...

My God they'd say...
we are the monsters in our midst...

They test, they do, in crisp white coats...
They do to save our lives...
to keep the humans in ever bliss
with pills to keep us well...

I ask you now...do we need this...

Do we need this…"for well?"
Cages and pained animals…
to keep us all so well…

We call it other names…we do…
We call it research and give it scientific acclaim…
Awards are made and honors given
as the pain of millions grow…

I ask you now…to consider this…
Consider it's all a lie…
We need no labs that bring this pain…
We need no labs that maim…

Walk in that door and see the pain
and ask your heart to speak…
It knows the answer…
though first may need to cry…
To cry…and wail…and wail and wail…
to see our precious ones caged…

The answers drip down your cheeks in tears…
The tears…O they do know…
Don't run in disgust
and pretend this is not…

O listen to your tears…
Stop this act…
Stop it now…
I can bear the pain no more…

We are the ones
who can stop the products of this pain…

We are the ones…
The feeling ones…
It's we who can say no to pain…

A culture of pain…
hidden behind closed doors…
It's time to open the doors…
The wailing will begin…

The animal pain is our pain…I say…
and our culture has inflicted the pain…

We are the wails of loving hearts
who couldn't stand to know…

This day is different…
We've opened the doors…
The animals…they go home…

Monsters in our midst no more…
O we can choose this day…

9-20-1997, pre-dawn in Mount Shasta, California

O Heaven World

And I come…bringing upon my back…
the lies that have been laid upon my head.
And I empty them back into the Void…
there to be washed clean
until disappeared as muddled mind
and reshaped into the Heaven World.

O Heaven World.
Be thou pouring through those who open and say yes…
O Heaven World.
Awaiting from faraway days…
dost thou weary of your waiting?

I am here.
Lest you leave…I shout into the Silence…
with unheard voice…
I am here.

I am here…
I am here and I breathe…
and borne upon my Soul…
is truth…and I sing…
I sing praises…
I sing the unsung praises in my Soul…

They have waited.
They have waited…
to be sung.

I carry endless songs and I carry endless love…
and I pour that love from out my heart…

A smile does form across my lips…
another day has passed…

5-22-1997, Mount Shasta, California

Seedless Society

Have we noticed that we've become
a culture who does not like seeds?

A culture who does not like seeds? What a metaphor!

We want seedless grapes, now seedless watermelon, and seedless oranges and tangelos and tangerines. Perhaps others will come soon. And will we buy that seedless fruit?

Seeds are the gifts of Life. The gifts of ongoing Life. And we are bothered by them, annoyed by them. They get in our way. We even want fast-food watermelon for the Fourth. We have bought it all.

We have failed to see the preciousness and sacredness of Life in the seed. Each seed we come across is an opportunity for sacred moment, to pause in prayer and gratitude. Each seed is a silent moment for reflection on the unmanifest. Each seed is a reflection of the Grand Silence.

And we are moving so fast, we hardly notice or remember that we have become a culture with no seeds. The seeds of Life. Our children will grow up with no respect for seeds. Maybe even no knowledge of seeds. We let the scientists hybrid them out. People cannot even collect their own seeds from this seedless food.

O how we deprive ourselves of the sacred symbols.

O how we deprive ourselves of meaning.

O how we live on the surface.

Now even removing the reflections that would take us from the visible to the invisible. These opportunities are ever around us and yet we support their disappearance. We support them by buying food that has been stripped of its seeds. To expand the metaphor, it would be like having a young woman stripped of her eggs and a man of his seeds. Yes, that is a stretch but that is the direction we are moving.

Let us pause a moment, reflect a moment, and be very clear what we will support. What we will buy. We are not just buying seedless fruit. We are buying a philosophy. And that way of life is sterile. It is devoid of Life!

And one person matters. You matter. I matter. We all matter. And what you do and I do touches and affects many…for generations to come.

> Give this day…a moment…to reflect on seeds!
> They are carriers.
> They are carriers of this Sacred Life.

11-6-1997, at dawn and pre-dawn in Mount Shasta, California

Fascinated with Pathologies

We are a nation fascinated with pathology.
We have become a nation fascinated with pathology.
We are fascinated with the pathology of the mind.
We are fascinated with the pathology of the emotions.
We are fascinated with pathology of the body.

We have made sciences of pathologies.
We give degrees in pathologies.
Pathologies of mind, emotion, and body.
BA's, Master's, and PhD's.
We have become doctors of pathology.
Scientists of pathology.
Pharmacists of pathology.

We talk about it.
We joke about it.
We laugh about it.
We cry about it.
We agonize about it.
We curse about it.
And we die of it.

And it…it is separation.
Separation from the guiding light.
Separation from true direction.
Separation from Spirit.

We are a nation fascinated with the separation from Spirit.
We are misguided.
We are living lies.
We are puppets of grand lies that have become institutions.

Imagine. We have institutionalized lies.
Pathologies are lies.
We are a nation fascinated with lies.
We even legalize prozac to cope with lies.
We are a land of lies.
We are dying of these lies.
And amid our midst, many minds begin to see.
They begin to see the lies.

They begin to ask. Why aren't we a happy healthy nation? Why have we associations for eyes and hearts and myriad other organs? Why are we a nation looking for new organs we have denigrated, that we have degenerated? Why have we lowered ourselves to raising and farming animals for their organs? Because we are sick. We have become a sick nation and no one wants to talk about it.

If we make sickness a science, charge a lot, and give it special names, we can be proud of it and discuss it over cocktails, destroying our liver.

We are a clever people. Most clever. We have made the science and the fascination cool. It is cool to be able to discuss the "ologies" and to discuss the medicine for mind, emotion, and body. And to be really up on the latest, greatest pharmaceuticals.

We have made these scientists kings! We have buried truth under chemicals. TV shows, movies are woven around the high drama of pathology. We are a nation who has mastered the drama of pathology. We sing about it, write about it, act about it.

We are the slaves of pathology.
And we are sick.
And we are stupid.
And it is shocking.

And we love to see how we can get away with separation. All to see how we can leave Source. Leave the Source of Truth. Leave for a stay…from a life that creates healthy mind, healthy emotion, healthy body.

We have left a life of simple.

We have left it for a life of coping with endless complexity. Pathologies are complexities woven from strands of separation. Minds and bodies coping with layer after layer of problems and related problems…on and on compounding themselves.

There are young people growing up, who are so ignorant of Truth, that they believe these lies are Life. They actually believe it is natural and normal to get sick, to get these diseases. They think it is natural to get even a cold or the flu. They are ways of life. They are household words. And they are the living lie. And it is sad. We are our own specimen of pathology. We are our own creation. We are the result of the living lie. And it is sad.

And there is another nation.
It is a parallel universe of people who have awakened.
They are awakening out of the lies.

They desire Truth.
And Truth comes.
Truth comes in books, in teachers, in ancient ways.
It comes in dreams.
It comes in the night.
And it sings.

It sings of a new day…
It sings of a new world.
It sings of unsought heights.

It sings beyond the hidden rage of humanity
that lies dismal in sophisticated creations of pathology.
It sings of solitude
where the madding crowd cannot be found.
It sings of peace.
Peace in the mind and peace in the emotions.
It sings of the way to this peace.

And this peace is the savior we all seek.
It dwells within.
It awaits our notice.
It comes with no fanfare, no degrees,
no conceited names, no snobbery, and no cool names.
It comes with no pathological fascination.

One must leave that fascination behind.
One must leave the libraries of books
that dwell in that sickness of fascination.

We must become empty.
And still.
And open our mind to Truth.
We must be open to the trickle of Truth.
We must be open to change.
We must be open to walking away
from society's foundation formed by lies.
We must not be caught up in the grieving mass.
We must simply, very simply…
walk away from the science of pathology…
We doctor lies…
while we can create truth.

Aren't we a funny species?
That we could become such a spectre?
And we think we are so advanced.

We are a pathetic civilization. We bought the lies. And millions make millions of dollars from our ignorance. You can be sure Truth will not be revealed from the sector of our population who make riches from the perpetuation of the lie. These deceitful or uninformed souls live in fear…in great fear…that Truth be known.

> Well…Truth…It comes.
> It comes…
> And it comes into the hearts and souls of those who ask.

> Is there another way?
> Is there a better way?
> What is the way?
> And for each, in their own way, that way is revealed.
> A journey out of the lie.

As the eyes clear…as the mind clears…one sees that no doctoring is needed. Just change. And regeneration. And purification. It may take time. But it is the way. Businesses, institutions, foundations, industry…they will need to fashion themselves anew.

For light is revealing itself and we cannot hide in the disguises of the lies. They are mockeries. And we grow weary of being sick. We even feign sick to stay home from this sick society. We even create sick to give us time off from the stress and struggle of a sick civilization. Or we drink to escape for even a moment…the depression of our collective creation.

We try to be proud of our creations. But lo, there is little to be proud of. And we drink to forget. If we can forget. For just a moment. And that moment merges with the next. Party after party…we forget our misery. Smiling into the next long-stemmed glass or the next talked-about vintage or the newest coolest brew.

Yes, we forget.
We forget the lie for a moment.
And we forget the Truth.
We enter the oblivion of forgetfulness.
At least the pain caused by the lie is gone.
Yes, the pain is gone.

We have become a society who knows how to avoid pain. But underneath the surface, everyone knows that pain is lurking… for pain is the child of a culture of lies. And no one wants to face that child.

And no one has to face that pain…if they should call for Truth. Truth shall disclose herself, unveil herself, and she shall dance before your eyes. And you shall see. You shall see the way. Truth is the way. We can call it Krishna, Jesus, Buddha, and on and on through all the messengers…but Truth is the way.

In the Silence…in the center of your Being…awaits Truth.
It awaits your notice.
One by one shall we enter the new world.
It is a lucid and clear state of consciousness.
And It awaits.

A new day comes.
And it is a world without end.
And it awaits our saying yes.
It awaits…for it Already Is.

12-31-1997, at 4:30 a.m. on New Year's Eve day
on retreat in Crestone, Colorado

Breakthrough into the Light

Talk shows, bestseller books and recordings, workshops, and videos are in ever larger numbers sharing potent spiritual stories of individual breakthroughs into the Light. People have been saved by the Light, embraced by the Light, loved by the Light, filled with the Light, led by the Light, and fully transformed by the Light. These stories are inspirational, powerful, educational, and fascinating…and all are deep and moving preparation for things to come in this decade and beyond.

People are walking away from accidents, surgeries, diseases, head-on collisions, lightning strikes, and all sorts of tragedies… sharing mystical stories of angels, beings of Light, a world beyond, and tales of "there is no death" and "there is only Love." The stories shared are greatly changing and shifting the collective consciousness. The collective is appearing now hungry for these stories of another Reality, as can be seen by the growing sales of these revelatory materials.

Each of us may now look carefully at the fascination and glamour that surrounds "breakthroughs into the Light via tragedy." Is that the collective pattern we desire to continue? Is that the collective story we want to create? Is it even the individual story we want to create? It is the story of human unconscious miscreation of the agonies of pain borne of separation from Source.

We have a conscious choice of moving, in non-tragic ways, into the "Planetary Initiation into the Oneness" that is upon us all. The question we may each ask is how we will choose to access the Light. How we will access our part of the One Global Vision seen in the Light?

How will we begin our passage into the Light of Knowing?

How will be begin our passage into the "once upon a non-time?"

Hopefully we will not continue to use tragedies as our collective access point. Ever people speak glowingly of how natural disasters, such as earthquakes, fires, and floods have pulled communities or nations together in Love. People share glowing stories of never knowing such profound Love, Light, and Oneness and unity.

What a sad commentary on our collective creation that we access love via disasters. It is a sad commentary on the human drama.

Each of us could be studying the plethora of information, ancient and new, that is available, to find what path suits us. Rich information abounds on living our lives in "consciousness beyond problems and troubles." We may live our lives in the Light.

We no longer need to create the near-death experiences of accidents, diseases, drugs, or tragedy to have breakthroughs into the Light.

The time is now for each to decide how we will access our individual and collective breakthroughs into the Light.

The time is now.

As a humanity, we may dedicate our lives to the Light of Knowing. That is the Light of love/wisdom married. Disasters shall end. We shall live the Oneness…for we are that very Light.

A Painless World Birth

together…we are birthing a new world…
together…we can have a painless birth…
together…we can "sound in" the new world…

I awoke this morning, at pre-dawn, as usual. I meditated on Grace, on the Presence of God, as usual. A building pressure from inside my Being ensued. Finally, a little after dawn, the words…

we can have a painless birth…

we can have a painless birth…

we can have a painless birth…

continued to repeat and repeat through my mind. I tried at first to remove the words, for that is not what I desired to write or think next. The words continued…as a mounting chant…a growing pressure intense within my mind. And finally I let it in. Consciousness, the One, has something I am to write. I have a busy day planned with art and sessions. This is not my agenda at all. But here goes…

Humanity can have a painless birth! Yes, we can have a painless birth. It is our choice. Together…it is our choice. There are ones that will have and are already having a painless birth. Individually, they have made their choice. And it is a painless birth.

Now is the time of the Collective Choice. The time is here. We are on the brink of birthing a new world. Everyone, everywhere is feeling the contractions of the new birth. That is where we are in the birthing process. We can have a long drawn-out painful birth or we can have an accelerated, exhalted, painless birth. It is our choice. Collectively we must make a choice. The media and technology has now prepared the way for the world to make Collective Choice almost simultaneously. The hundredth monkey syndrome is firmly in place.

together…we are birthing a new world…

together…we can have a painless birth…

together…we can "sound in" the new world…

it is our choice…

I must tell a story. It is an important story. It is a shard of Her-story in His-story. It is a true story. It is part of the True-story which woman-She has to share upon this time. In 1975, I had a painless birth.

I had a painless birth.

No one at that time wanted to hear my story. Even most women did not want to hear my story. They wanted to repeat and repeat the stories of their painful birth…the hours, the days, the drama, the sweat and tears. I could not understand at the time why others did not want to hear my ecstatic story of a painless birth. At that time, I thought my story was only about a painless childbirth. I had no idea that it was about a painless world-birth. I had much growing, learning, and sounding ahead.

It is time for us to understand the metaphor of woman-birth.

It is the metaphor for world-birth. It is the metaphor for all-birth.

It is a mind-staggering metaphor.

I will tell the birth story so the metaphor I share is understood.

In 1975, I was pregnant with my second child. After a conventional, horrible, hospital first birth, lying unnaturally on my back, with feet in stirrups, no nurses or doctors with any offerings of help during painful contractions in the lonely labor room…I was fearful about this second birth. Even my husband had refused to be there for the first birth. He never did say why. And I chose a spinal injection because I was too tight and so scared and the desire to be painless was so strong. So while I was now numbed to physical pain, the emotional pain was deep and overwhelming. The entire birth was many hours and can only be described as an ordeal. Sad, but very true.

So I was well experienced and prepared to make a new choice of birth. I read every book I could find on natural childbirth and took all the breathing and exercise classes for pregnant women. Because of my first birth, I still had the residue of lingering fear, so I covered my past painful act by having a doctor and a nurse at the natural home birth. They were my "just in case act." I had also been in touch with a wonderful midwife the entire pregnancy. She was there.

So the day arrived in the Fall of 1975 for the birth of my second daughter. It was mid-morning and I was at a local market. I felt an unusual feeling in my womb, and intuitively I knew it was time. I walked home, called the doctor and midwife, and placed myself on my bed, amidst pillows, candles, and Yogananda chants. The home birth stage was set. It was simple. I remember moving all about, finding my perfect position of comfort outside, that matched the feelings inside. Then everyone arrived and I was ready.

My first daughter was now five and wanted so to be there. I did not call her at school because I still had vestiges of fear from my first birth, and in case my natural childbirth was not as graceful as the hundreds I had read about, I did not want to pass on to her that picture of childbirth. I did not have full confidence of a painless birth. I was deeply sad that I did not know if I could give her a beautiful experience.

The next thing that happened changed the birth, my world, and my life. I spontaneously began to make sounds. The midwife realized the importance of the unusual sounds and began to make even louder ones than me. That single act of hers broke my inhibition of really going for it, which I did.

While I was making these sounds, from deep within my being, I began to have this amazing inner experience. It was as if I were "riding a sound ray." As long as I made the sounds, I had no pain. It was ecstatic. It was like watching the birth from the inside, while having the birth on the outside. I was both a guest at the event, as well as being the event. It was like riding the "edge of paradox." Was I inside or outside? I was both.

As long as I made the loud, other-worldly sounds, not only did I have no pain, but my body began to easily position and posture itself from within as the birth progressed. I allowed. I became fluid. I never even needed to push. The contractions do it all. The birth just happens? I was the beholder of this wondrous event. Blessed! I just needed to breathe, open, and sound! Even at the crowning of the head, I announced the name of the new daughter; it was not the name I had chosen.

At her crowning, I announced, "Her name is Rebecca Rachael." No one yet knew if the baby was male or female. I had done no tests. The feeling from inside my body was as if her Soul Consciousness said "now" and she simply projected herself into the world. My body was by then positioned at an angle, like a runway, and she came in for a landing from Infinity. The entire birth was about an hour…painless…when I would make the sounds from my Soul.

Now, I would have thought nothing more about it, except that the sounds, along with beautiful, very free-flowing movements and body configurations, continued to want to birth through me. And I allowed. And the metaphor of world-birth emerged.

This sharing is not intended to give the details of all the tones, the sounds, the movements, the visions, and information that have continued to come forth since 1975. It is intended to share just enough to give the feeling for what doing soul sounds can do for the planetary birthing now happening. For I learned, as I continued this journey in the Sounds and Signings of the Soul, that it was about "all birthing."

It is so utterly simple, as to go unobserved and unnoticed and unrealized. The woman-story, Her-story, has much to share about birthing. We are the birthers. Our metaphorical stories must be heeded if we are to divert catastrophe for the collective. We can choose a painless birth.

As I continued the sounds, I read esoteric and metaphysical books about Sacred Sounds. All that was happening through me was being confirmed in all the information from ancient knowledge. I began to feel like an ancient-birth. For as time went on, I could feel the Soul Sounds open me up to new realities, new dimensions, new knowings…that were really ancient knowings, Ancient Rememberings. I realized that my experiences in childbirth had actually "birthed me" into a new reality.

The shifts I refer to are bigger than paradigm shifts. They are from the mind-less realm. They are from the Silence. They are from the timeless. The sounds opened me to feel my unbridled, natural, and unlimited Self. The sounds and movements were realized as a portal into the Infinite. What I would do with what I saw is another story.

I could write an entire book, just on the experiences that I have had in the years of doing Sounds of the Soul…alone, with individuals, with groups, as presentations, and doing the sounds pre-dawn, day, dusk, and night. Doing sounding with rocks, waterfalls, and on and on.

I learned to play my own polarity between masculine and feminine with sound. I grew to love both aspects. I learned to facilitate others to access their Soul Sounds and Movements. I learned to play the polarity with them and for them. I learned to feel the subtlest of energies of Creator, as they became the Dance of He and She, the dance of God as man and woman. And I learned to be aware of them through all of Nature.

I began to have cosmic glimpses and experiences into other dimensions and realms. I began to deeply feel Grace and feel the Presence. I began to know the human body as the Temple Template of Infinity, from the inner planes. I began to sit at the "edge of paradox" in meditation, the place in Consciousness that beholds Creation.

The new world that is being birthed is in our Consciousness. We are birthing a new Consciousness. We are collectively birthing a realized world beyond the senses. And it can happen painlessly through sounding. The sounds at first are tones. Tones still the mind, balance one's energy, open one to the subtle realms. It is literally like the "parting of the Red Sea." It opens up the three dimensional world and allows one to know and feel and see into other dimensions. And realize…there is no separation.

Once the 3-D world is opened up, one can begin to hear the angelic realms and the celestial realms and the profound music of the spheres. One will only want to listen to the inner recordings!

I have had visions of the entire planet sounding. Sounding the Call of Creation…that we are all One. One mind, One Soul, One being. The memories, the Ancient Rememberings that we are One, are all there.

> together…we can remember…
>
> together…we can remember that we are One…

Once the tones are used to open up the 3-D, the Soul Sounds from the higher realms actually can play through the listener. The ecstasy, the rapture, the joy are beyond what words could ever say. And the experiences that I am describing are like having an orgasm, only beyond orgasm, like having that flash of Oneness, of merging, only staying there…having that place in Consciousness sustained and maintained.

When I hear people talk of a collapsing economy, I remind them that forms and structures that do not serve this new world are changing, shifting and that if they will look around they will see as many new forms birthing. We must be flexible and fluid in these times and the toning and sounding from the Center of one's being can and will facilitate that shift.

> Again we have the choice.

Many have already made the choice and their individual transition is moving smoothly. I offer these words and these experiences, that others may know that All can sound from the center of their being where resides the One God, Source, the Creator and begin to open to our interrelatedness, to our interconnectedness.

the One and the many…

the One and the same…

There are many people now facilitating others to sound and tone from the Soul. You may choose someone who will "midwife" you through your part of the World-Birth. Choose someone who can show you how to have a painless birth. Choose someone who can teach you how to do it on your own. Choose someone who will remind you to have direct communion with God, with Source. No separation.

We have entered a time that allows the choice of no intercessors, that is, no mediums, no readers, no channels, no priests, no preachers. We have entered a time to prepare for direct knowing. A deep realization of our Oneness.

It is our choice.

The birthing metaphor is critical at this time of the planetary unfoldment. Woman-birthing is the metaphor for "all-birthing." We can learn from natural childbirth how to do the world-birth.

The man-world of the Western culture has shared much about how to make the shift into the new world. But little has been shared about how to have a painless birth. And little has been shared by technology of how to "access visions of the new world." It has been said by awakened ones, that people and nations with no vision will perish. History has proved it.

Millions around this world are waking up. Should we begin to

"Sound the Call of Creation" together, we will together "sit at the edge of paradox," at the crack in the universe and behold Creation.

Sounding a painless birth is a part of the woman-story. Her-story of this new world. Sounding from the center of one's being dissolves the pain of the creation of human emotions. It actually dissolves the miscreated emotions. Only the emotion of God, ecstasy, and feelings of unlimited imagination, can arise. When miscreated emotions are gone, access to God's Plan is opened wide. We are then ready to see what we were not ready to see. For pain blocked the view.

In this new world, which starts in the Consciousness, we will see Balance. As man and woman together, attune to the center of their being, to the Presence of the One God, and begin to sound, a new world will birth. And it is a painless birth.

Let us behold home-mother and home-father make the passage into world-mother and world-father and together birth a new world.

The sounds of man and woman will create a fusion, a resonance of unprecedented splendor. That Dance of HE and SHE, done first with sounds, will lead to orgasms of consciousness that comes from the wordless and the nameless.

Again, we have the choice.

Let us this day choose a painless birth.

When this message was complete, I found myself looking through old journals. I came to Christmas Eve, 1988. In meditation that eve, the planet was revealed to me, birthed into the Christ child. It included everything on the planet, as one mind, one body, one Being.

On January 1, 1989, the birthing message continued. Inwardly, I heard:

> See the Kingdom everywhere.
> See everywhere…
> the endless formations of God…
> the endless formations of Infinity…
> the endless formations of the Two as One…
> the endless formations of He and She…

As the days went by, the birthing message continued. I reread Ken Carey's *Return of the Bird Tribes*. He informed us eloquently that the planet is a single living entity, a Being. I now really understood. What was revealed in the Christmas Eve meditation was where we are in the world birth. The gestation period of the pregnancy is complete. The body evolution is complete. All organs and body parts and cells are fully formed. We are now ready for the birth, ready for labor and the birth canal, and ready to move collectively into the fourth dimension and beyond. And together, during the contractions, we can sound. We can sound from our very soul. And we can allow the movements…the dance of the soul.

> Together…we can sound from the One Soul…

We are birthing a new consciousness, a soul Consciousness. We will learn to "see the Kingdom Everywhere." We shall experience…together…the OmniPresence. It is our shifting consciousness that allows this world birth to happen painlessly. A shift in consciousness, to focus on the One Mind, allows a transparent mind. That human no-mind space creates an opening to the One Mind. It is this opening though which the World Birth is happening now.

and together…we can have a painless birth…

together…we can "sound in" the new world…

11-6-1997, Mount Shasta, California

Marie Saint-Marie: Mystic Artist, Writer, and Spiritual Educator

Mary Saint-Marie is a mystic artist, writer, poet, and spiritual educator. *Nectar of Woman* follows two previous books, *Galactic Shamanism* and *The Holy Sight* and two recordings. The recordings are *She…it is…who Remembers* and *Return to Oneness*.

From her mountain retreat, Mary has traveled extensively with her art exhibits nationwide, doing over 150 showings. She has also traveled nationwide with Soul Sessions, Soul Retreats, and multi-media enactments inspiring others into the awareness of Oneness, the Presence, that each may express their true essence. She describes the work as The Mystical as Practical.

Mary wrote a play, *The Monitor and Laughter of the Gods,* that was performed as sacred theatre in the well-known theatre destination, Ashland, Oregon. She also wrote a book of new earth parables gently guiding others into "the garden that already IS." The book is *The Oracle and the Dreamer*.

The mystical, sacred, and visionary art of Mary Saint-Marie is inspirational and mirrors our oneness with Creator/Creation. It is a reflection of the marriage of earth and sky. It is a reflection of our true essence, our true identity as the One. It depicts the holy.

The Art-of-the-Soul is a journey into the land of Archetypal realms of wholeness. The paintings are witness to the Law of Balance in all of nature that is the law of love.

The paintings are multi-media, multi-technique, and multi-dimensional. The mixed media effects and multi-layerings create a soul depth of the primordial and eternal Star Stone Essence. Revealed is Life As Living Ceremony.

Mary's luminous body of work has appeared on cards, cds, calendars, and magazines, such as *Quest* and *Mystic Pop*. Mary's work may be found in *One Source Sacred Journeys, Songs from the Edge of Everything,* and *The Ways of Spirit*. Mary and her Art-of-the-Soul have also appeared on television nationwide and in Germany. Most recently Mary's art has been featured in the movie FEMME, a powerful film revealing the voice of the divine feminine through many women of the world.

Mary has been pioneering art exhibitions that reveal universal principles of Oneness and the divine feminine since 1972 in galleries, conferences, symposiums, expositions, faires, workshops and retreats.

The art of Mary Saint-Marie is collected nationally and internationally.

* Art collectors, buyers and art lovers are invited to Mary's website and to her three art books. The art books represent three separate phases of the artist's reflection of the eternal, the I Am Awareness.

The books are: *The Sacred Two, The Star-Stone Ones,* and *Art As Consciousness*.

Mystic Art, Books, Sessions, and Retreats

Mystic Art

Fine Art Giclee Reproductions are available.

Inquire about original art.

Books

Books may be ordered on Amazon.

Galactic Shamanism
The Sacred Two
The Holy Sight
Nectar of Woman
Messages from the Silence
The Star-Stone Two
The Animating Presence
The Monitor and Laughter of the Gods
Art as Consciousness
The Oracle and the Dreamer

CDs

Soul Sounds of World Birth
Journey of Consciousness

Website gives more information about:
Mystic Art
Soul Sessions
Soul Retreats
Holy Sight workshops

Note the youtube videos and interviews.

www.marysaintmarie.com
www.EarthCareGlobalTV.com

www.ingramcontent.com/pod-product-compliance
Lightning Source LLC
Chambersburg PA
CBHW050647160426
43194CB00010B/1842